The right of Lyndsay King to be identified as the author of this work has been asserted by her in accordance with the Copyright, Designs and Patent Act 1998

Published by

The Mountain Training Trust - 2006

Copyright - Mountain Training Trust

ISBN 978-0-9554675-0-9

The Central Council of Physical Recreation, of which I became President in 1951, was founded by Phyllis Colson in 1934 as an association of the national governing bodies of sports and recreations. One of its major purposes was to promote public participation in sports and recreations. Together with the respective governing bodies, it established two National Recreation Centres; at Lilleshall, initially for athletics, football, and gymnastics, and at Bisham Abbey for tennis, netball, cricket and sailing. It later established a National Sailing Centre at Cowes. There still remained the need to satisfy the strong demand for a national centre for mountaineering and outdoor recreation. In the early 1950s, the old Royal Hotel near Capel Curig was acquired and re-named Plas y Brenin.

This book tells the story of the inception and development of Plas y Brenin. It is quite a dramatic story of ups and downs, but, I am glad to say, it has a happy ending. After 50 years, it has become fully established as the National Mountain Centre and is managed by a charity, the Mountain Training Trust, on behalf of the key national governing bodies .

Contents

Acknowledgements

My thanks to everyone at Plas y Brenin who has patiently dealt with myriad questions without complain
Also particularly to Ian Wall, who conceived the project and undertook a large amount of personal researc
that ultimately made my task easier as it helped to signpost my own research route. Listing every individua
who has offered guidance or shared memories would take several pages but the following have made notabl
contributions that were very much appreciated -

Di Airey

Dave Alcock

Mary Astrid Ayers

John Barry

Pete Catterall

Dave Cheetham

Loel Collins

John Cousins

Malcolm Creasey

Harry Cropper

Norman Croucher

John Disley

Martin Doyle

Ann Dwyer

Ken Dwyer

K C Gordon

Jean Hayward

Pat Hobby

Issie Inglis

Eileen Jackson

John Jackson

Barbara James

Ann Jones

Doug Jones

Gordon Jones

Paddy Jones

Sheila Leitch (née Deans)

Derek Mayes

Gim Milton

Roger Orgill

Iain Peter

Robert Pettigrew

Simon Powell

Teresa Ruewell

Anne Salisbury

Rob Spencer

Joyce Stock

Louise Thomas

Twid Turner

Derek Walker

Photographers:

With thanks to all who kindly contributed their photographss:

Chris Bonington, Dave Cheetham, Loel Collins, John Disley, Martin Doyle, Phil Dowthwaite, Carlo Forte, Ruth Greenal, Robin Jackson, Kendal Film Festival Archive, Steve Long, Stuart McAleese, Twid Turner and the Plas y Brenin Archive.

Introduction

The 50th anniversary of the founding of Plas y Brenin seemed the ideal time to consider putting together a history of the Centre. However, embarking on such a project brought up matters for immediate consideration. Should it be light-hearted with the risk that both the book and consequently Plas y Brenin will be seen as lightweight by those with little knowledge about the outdoors? Should it be intensely detailed, where the risk is that it will be a dry, dusty tome that no-one ever takes down from the shelf and actually reads? Our primary criteria was to find a balance where this book would not only be informative for those with little knowledge or understanding about the development of outdoor pursuits in the UK, but it would also be an entertaining read for those who know Plas y Brenin intimately.

The obvious compromise in aiming for a publication that is interesting reading without being a weighty tome, is that it is absolutely impossible to mention every single event or person associated with Plas y Brenin over the past 50 years. Sometimes, this is because things have genuinely slipped through the net when we have been researching; sometimes it is because it has proved impossible to clarify something; more often, it is because there simply isn't space to include everything. What it never is, is a deliberate exclusion.

I hope you feel that, overall, the balance is right and that we have accurately represented all that Plas y Brenin is, and was, throughout the last 50 years. Above all, I hope we have captured the spirit of the people - students, staff, friends - who have all helped to make Plas y Brenin unique.

One day, I am sure, Plas y Brenin will be celebrating its centenary - perhaps we should start collecting memories now.

Iain Peter

A Child of its Time

At the midpoint of the 20th century, mountaineering was still perceived as something of an elite activity. For many, it was associated only with the major expeditions and Everest had yet to be conquered. But there was a growing gravitation towards the hills as it was recognised that they held a wealth of opportunity in terms of recreation. As a result, perceptions changed rapidly.

Within 50 years, hill walking became one of the most popular leisure activities, and outdoor education grew to become a routine part of the national curriculum. That change was possible, at least in part, because of the transformation of everything surrounding the industry - the establishment of training and recognisable standardised qualifications, the growth of centres, the development of courses and the improvement in the status of those involved. Nowadays, outdoor educators expect to have input into matters of importance that are not immediately seen as within their purview - the Work at Height Regulations, the Countryside and Rights of Way Act 2000, the rise of the "compensation culture" etc. No longer are those with the knowledge and experience to make a notable contribution marginalised or ignored.

Plas y Brenin has played a prominent role in these advances over the last 50 years, but its establishment owes much to the changes in attitude over the decades preceding its opening, and the vision and hard work of a determined group of individuals.

Many of the organisations that are so familiar today were relatively new in the 1950s. Even the Scouts and irl Guides had not yet reached their 50th anniversary, while the outh Hostels Association and Outward Bound were much younger.

The change came quickly - those born in the 1950s and 1960s were resented with activities such as hill walking as a matter of course, and some schools were already developing climbing walls and combining outdoor education with normal PE activities, broadening the range offered to pupils.

The Central Council for Physical Recreation (CCPR) was established in England in 1934 as the Central Council of Representative Physical Training. It's primary purpose was to 'bring home the benefits of physical culture'. It was extended to encompass Scotland and Wales with a further extension to include Northern Ireland in 1949. In 1943, the CCPR set up the Outdoor Activity Advisory Committee (OAAC).

The idea that mountaineering could be taught and that teaching could be available to everyone was, at the time, revolutionary, and contributed to the surge of interest. Kurt Hahn was instrumental in the setting up of Outward Bound, with the Aberdovey Sea School opening during the war years. 1948 was an eventful year - the Scottish Sports Council opened Glenmore Lodge, near Aviemore; the Welsh Office ran what was probably the first rock climbing course for the CCPR, with students staying at Capel Curig and Idwal Cottage Youth Hostels. And the same year, Nea Morin and Evelyn Leach ran the CCPR's first mountaineering course for girls, also in Snowdonia. By 1951, Derbyshire had become the first local education authority to set up its own Centre for Open Country Pursuits at White Hall, near Buxton. By 1953, organisations that were instrumental and influential in the development of outdoor education had become members of the OAAC - the British Mountaineering Council, Outward Bound and the National Association of Youth Officers. This unity gave the visionaries the opportunity to work together and they took it.

The individuals involved were as important as the organisations, with many of their names being familiar to successive generations without them necessarily being able to pinpoint their role in the development of the facilities available today. Jack Longland (knighted in 1970), who recognised the need for training associated with mountaineering and who was the driving force behind the creation of White Hall; Eric Shipton, Warden of Eskdale Outward Bound; Nea Morin, who helped to pioneer women's mountaineering; Sir John Hunt (later Lord Hunt of Llanfair Waterdine), leader of the expedition that achieved the first ascent of Everest in 1953, and his deputy on that expedition, Dr Charles Evans (knighted in 1969); Geoffrey Winthrop Young, whose vision saw the creation of the British Mountaineering Council. All devoted energy to creating opportunities for all to share

The setting of Plas y Brenin:

". . . we come in sight of Capel Curig, the many peaks of Snowdon, the Wyddfa crowned as it so often is, alone among its satellites even upon the clearest days, with a wreath of fluffy cloud, break finely across the western sky. Some scattered cottages, an ancient little church, and a big hotel looking down upon two sparkling lakes and up a bare green valley towards Snowdon is all that there is of the far-famed village of Capel Curig. And the big hotel must not be contemptuously brushed aside as a mere excresence of modern travel. For in an old engraving that lies before me bearing the date of nearly a century ago, it stands out as large to all seeming as it is today."

Highways and Byways of North Wales by A G Bradley, illustrated by Joseph Pennell and Hugh Thomson, pp 251-2, pub MacMillan & Co Ltd 1901

in the adventure offered by Britain' countryside and were taken seriousl because of their own achievements.

Alongside the newly establishec centres, the CCPR ran courses from several bases, working closely witl the national bodies governing a variety of outdoor activities including cycling, sailing and canoeing. By the early 1950s, Glenmore Lodge was already expanding to run mountaineering courses in Northern Ireland, Snowdonia, the Lake District and the Peak District. And it was obvious there was sufficient interest in the activities offered for there to be room for growth in this fledgling field. It was a natural progression to establish a second mountaineering centre elsewhere.

Sir John Hunt points out the route to a group of trainee leaders from the expedition section of the Duke of Edingurgh's Award Scheme - circa 1959

But acceptance of the idea was not enough. Funding was also required.

The Whitbread Sports Fund was established specifically to promote outdoor activities and granted bursaries for people wanting to attend training courses. But this funding was not sufficient to set up and maintain an entire centre.

In 1952, when King George VI died, a Memorial Fund was established. Because of the late King's interest in the improvement of leisure facilities, the CCPR decided that the expansion of National Recreation Centres in the UK would be a worthy memorial to a monarch who had been much loved and was long perceived to have been in touch with his people. Two centres already existed - Bisham Abbey for tennis, netball, cricket and sailing and Lilleshall for athletics, football and gymnastics. So the focus was on a centre for mountaineering and other outdoor activities and, in March 1954, it was announced that the King George VI Memorial Fund was setting aside £400,000 for the establishment of National Recreation Centres. Sixty thousand pounds of this money was specifically for the Snowdonia mountaineering centre.

The King's death inadvertently raised public awareness of mountaineering in a way that could not have been predicted. In 1953, on the day of Queen Elizabeth II's coronation, news reached the UK of the success of Sir John Hunt's Everest expedition - for the first time, the summit of the world's highest mountain had been reached and the media reported on the coronation with "all this and Everest too". The euphoria of a nation recovering from the war years and facing a new era widened to encompass that achievement. The opportunity to develop outdoor education was never going to be riper.

It took some time to find suitable premises and many locations were visited, including the Lake District and other sites in North Wales - Bala, Dolgellau and along the coast. One driving force was Phyllis Colson, whose vision and commitment were inspired, while the search was co-ordinated by Justin Evans, Deputy Secretary and Acting General Secretary of the CCPR. He discovered, via John Disley, that the Royal Hotel in Capel Curig, ight in the heart of Snowdonia, was about to come onto the market and he met with the owner, Eugene Brunning.

Capel Curig was renowned for its harp making in the 17th century. The flora of the area had encouraged exploration by early botanists, with Thomas Johnston visiting in 1639. Thomas Pennant raised awareness of Snowdonia when he wrote "Tours of Wales" in 1778 and J M W Turner was amongst artists drawn to its beauty in the early 19th century.

The Royal Hotel had originally been the Capel Curig Inn, opened around 1801 by Richard Pennant, the owner of the Penrhyn Quarry, to accommodate those first tourists after a road was built from Bethesda. A short time later the London to Holyhead turnpike was completed and brought more travellers. While the road itself followed the route of the modern A5 through the Ogwen Valley fairly closely, the hotel's location was dictated by the dramatic views offered from the shores of Llynnau Mymbyr. From the hotel - on a clear day - there was a stunning view of the Snowdon Horseshoe to the west and Moel Siabod rose from the hotel grounds to the south. Whilst Capel Curig has never grown in size the way some of the neighbouring villages have, it quickly became a tourist centre. The road was improved and, within eight years of the Capel Curig Inn opening, the mail coach was re-routed from the coastal route. Shortly after that, the road was improved by Thomas Telford, whose influence can still be seen today in the line of the A5 and the bridging of the Menai Straits. The hotel's name was changed in the 1850's to the Capel Curig Hotel and changed again to the Royal Hotel in the 1870s after playing host to several members of the royal family, including Queen Victoria, who was among the guests who signed window panes. Apart from a few years when it was used as a training centre for mountain warfare during World War II, the building remained in use as a hotel for over 150 years. By the time it closed there were three other hotels in Capel Curig, all popular with the climbing fraternity.

So it was that a purchase was negotiated, within the CCPR's budget and to include all fixtures and fittings. Eugene

Guests enjoying afternoon tea outside the Royal Hotel

Brunning retained some land and buildings, which became known as the "Annexe", consisting of a strip of land along the riverside with a cottage, a house, domestic quarters and a paddock. There were also several tenants in situ - Chester Mountaineering Club, the Royal British Legion and a wool shop all had quarters on the site and were to remain there for some years.

The Royal Hotel became Plas y Brenin - the King's House - the Snowdonia National Recreational Centre, and the focus moved to how the Centre was to be run. The CCPR decided that the Centre should have its own full time staff, rather than teaching staff visiting when required, as the level of expertise envisaged made that necessary. Major G I "Gim" Milton was appointed as the first Warden and took up his post in July 1955. His Chief Instructor was John Disley, who had two assistants - Roger Orgill and Tim Aron. Surveyors Cook and Arkwright were employed to supervise the many alterations necessary to provide the facilities required, with the Centre opening for business before they were all complete.

The CCPR had been advised to retain the hotel manager, Emrys Roberts, and he became the Centre's Bursar, remaining in post until 1968. Having a local on the staff helped enormously as it was important that the new Centre integrated into its community - local links had to be created and maintained for the venture to succeed. Emrys Roberts introduced Gim Milton to every farmer in the vicinity, establishing personal contact from the Centre's earliest days and erasing many of the problems that could have arisen over matters such as access. As a mark of appreciation of their neighbours, Plas y Brenin organised an annual Farmers' Night dinner, which was enjoyed by all. Although this tradition did cease, it was reintroduced in the 1990s by Iain Peter and has once again become a highlight in Plas y Brenin's social calendar and continues to build strong links with the community.

A Management Committee was set up and the members were familiar names to the mountaineering world. Sir John Hunt was the first Chairman. Sir Charles Evans, Mansel Williams (Caernarfon's Director of Education), J B Henderson (Chairman of the OAAC), Hayden Davies HMI (who represented the CCPR's Welsh Committee) and representatives from the BMC. The National Ski Federation of Great Britain was later also represented.

On 24 November 1955 at Plas y Brenin, the Management Committee met for the first time under the terms of reference -

"To undertake the general responsibilities for the management of Plas y Brenin National Recreation Centre, including the appointment of staff on salary scales laid down by the General Purposes and Finance Committee. The Committee shall submit general reports to the Executive Committee. On questions of finance, it should refer directly to the General Purposes and Finance Committee but shall have the authority to incur non-recurring expenditure not exceeding £100 on any one item without prior reference to that Committee."

The first events at Plas y Brenin had already taken place. They started with a CCPR Senior Staff Conference, which took place on 6-8 June 1955. This was closely followed by an Outward Bound course for girls, run by Ruth Keeble. In December, Gim Milton, Tim Aron and Roger Orgill paid a visit to Glenmore Lodge, returning with ideas and increased enthusiasm.

The gestation period was over and the birth of Plas y Brenin had been relatively uncomplicated. Now the nurturing began.

A Jewel in the Making

An 'away course' with students from NE Region in Borrowdale 1962. Centre front is David Humpheries, who prior to joining Plas y Brenin staff served as Chief Instructor to J.E.B Wright of the Montaineering Association, training some 15,000 people in rock climbing skills over its 20 years prior to absorption into the YHA. David went on to serve as MLTB Secretary, bringing much first-hand experience of the scheme to the then London-based administration.

No matter how well the groundwork had been done prior to the opening, as with any venture, success was not guaranteed, particularly when it was in such a new direction. But perhaps even the vision of the most enthusiastic supporters of Plas y Brenin never anticipated the overwhelming success it was to become; a place with a reputation for unequalled excellence that attracted students from across the globe while still being able to provide the most basic grounding in activities for the youngest members of its local community. And it was not only the students who recognised its worth, for many instructors being able to put Plas y Brenin on their CV proved to be a valuable tool in opening doors in their future careers. The Centre has not only fulfilled all expectations but has become the benchmark others are judged by.

But in the earliest days, to succeed, the CCPR had to ensure that people became aware of what their new Centre was offering. Their links with so many other organisations simplified this in terms of the actual advertising required, but there was still a degree of suspicion about non-

PLAS Y BRENIN   THE SNOWDONIA NATIONAL RECREATION CENTRE CAPEL CURIG, NORTH WALES

competitive activities.

The earliest days:

"We started that year with 40 students and a programme designed by John Disley which remained an excellent programme for the next five years. We soon realised that 40 students were not economic for the Centre financially so we decided that we would run two specialist courses for 10 students each making the total number up to 60. One was a rock climbing course designed and run by John Disley which was extremely popular and then there were conoeing courses in canoe/camping, sea canoeing and suchlike."

G I "Gim" Milton

2005

The team-building courses familiar to later generations of outdoor educators were yet to be devised, and the concentration was on teaching students how to climb and canoe and enabling others to do the same. Resources were limited. Post-war rationing had only recently been lifted and many items were still in short supply or had restrictions on their availability.

So it was that the canoe fleet consisted of just one double and one single canoe - hardly adequate for groups of 10 students. Capel Curig resident Owen Wyn Owen, an engineering lecturer at Bangor Technical College, built the first canoe trailer for the Centre and assisted where he could elsewhere. He remains a supporter of Plas y Brenin to this day and, like Emrys Roberts, has always been a strong link with the local community. Both Emrys and Owen Wyn provided invaluable help with the establishment of the fly-fishing courses, particularly with recruiting suitable VIs for the four to six courses each year. The instructor/student ratio was low - just 1:10 - so the courses provided much needed income in the early days. Some climbing equipment was provided, and, in case there was not enough interest in these "new" activities, the CCPR also supplied Plas y Brenin with a range of athletic and archery equipment, which remained stored at the Centre until the late 1960s.

The Whitbread Sports Fund was of enormous help over many years. Most of the Fund's grants were to prime new projects, but they also helped to maintain several. Items as diverse as a stable block (later converted to a rock climbing practice room), the construction of a boat for fly-fishing on Llynnau Mymbyr, a mountain flora garden and a film camera were paid for with Whitbread grants. The Fund also created a Bursary to enable physical education students to attend one week training courses, usually in December when the Centre would

Early kayaking course on Llynnau Mymbyr

therwise be very quiet. The bursaries continued for many years and, from 1964, they were modified to ake account of the new Mountain Leader Certificate MLC). With an average of 40 students benefiting rom the funding each year, three quarters took an MLC Introductory course and the remainder the Assessment.

In 1959, past bursary recipients were surveyed to see if they were contributing to the development of outdoor education. Of 78 students who attended the courses in 1956 and 1957, 60 responded to the questionnaires, with half of them stating that they were helping at the schools where they taught. Thirty-seven former students were taking part in activities themselves with one or two having returned to Plas y Brenin to work as Volunteer Instructors (VIs).

Horse riding was introduced in the 1950s

There were also grants from elsewhere - the Ministry of Education (and its successor, the Department of Education and Science) gave them for the installation of central heating and towards the construction of artificial ski facilities and work on staff cottages, as well as more general maintenance grants via the CCPR. Over a decade later some funding was still sourced from the Ministry, including the capital for the heated training pool and the cross-country ski track. In 1958 the Dulverton Trust gave £1,000 towards "running expenses" at Plas y Brenin and the National Sports Development Fund provided a grant in 1970. Without these monies Plas y Brenin would have developed at a much slower pace.

Initially, Plas y Brenin was open only seasonally with a student limit of 45 - increased to 60 later - and 350 students took part in the courses during its first season. They experienced hill-walking, navigation, camping, rock climbing and canoeing. There were even "away" courses on the earliest programmes - Gim Milton and Roger Orgill took students on a week long canoe tour of Welsh rivers. There was also a canoe camping course around Anglesey and the Menai Straits.

The Annual Report for 1956-7 states that the number of day sessions had nearly doubled from the previous year, with a total of 1,837 students attending for mountain activity training - 1,238 male and 599 female. By 1961, the number of day persons had risen to 16,619 and a decade later the figure stood at 17,084. There was a dip in the first half of the 1960s, almost certainly as a result of the rapid expansion of outdoor education with a rise in LEA centres, but Plas y Brenin quickly recovered. Overall, Centre usage always remained high, often over 90%, but this was only calculated for the time it was actually open.

Already, the Centre was expanding. Sheila Deans joined the permanent staff as the first female instructor, moving from Glenmore Lodge and remaining in post for three years. The programme was enlarged and quickly included winter mountaineering and field studies alongside some rather less well known OE activities alongside fly-fishing, "underwater swimming" and local history and legend. Gim Milton wanted to introduce riding - he was a keen horseman himself. Other activities were considered, and, while some were felt to be

1950's Pony Trekking course approaching St. Julietta Chapel

unviable, some were offered for short period and abandoned as they became outdated or under subscribed.

In 1956 the children of Ysgol Capel Curig came to Plas y Brenin to mark the visit of HRH Prince Philip for a belated opening of the Centre. It was the year the Duke of Edinburgh's Award Scheme was inaugurated and the Scheme shared its Chairman - Sir John Hunt - with the Plas y Brenin Management Committee. The Prince was a staunch supporter of Outward Bound and an important ally, widely recognised and known to have strong views on the use of the outdoors in the development of individuals. Plas y Brenin's close affinity with the Duke of Edinburgh's Award Scheme resulted in the Centre running a course for Award leaders and potential leaders in the summer of 1958. This connection remains to the present day as similar courses are still included in the programme. In 2005, the Duke of Edinburgh returned to Plas y Brenin to help to mark the 50th anniversary of the Centre.

In 1957, John Disley left and was replaced by John "Jacko" Jackson, who became Deputy Warden and Chief Instructor. It was the start of a 17 year connection with Plas y Brenin, during which its entire ethos crystallised and became the model on which many other centres were later based.

Prince Phillip visits a rock climbing session at the Pinnacles in 1956

Sir John Hunt was not trying to clone Outward Bound. Indeed, his views on the delivery of education through the medium of the outdoors were not in complete agreement with Kurt Hahn's. While the Outward Bound model was working well - and continues to do so to this day with the Trust thriving across the globe - Sir John found that his vision was more closely married to that of John Jackson. Prior to his appointment, Jackson had been a science and geography teacher who led his students on many expeditions into the hills. But he had also built up an impressive mountaineering resumé in the post-war years. John was a reserve climber for the 1953 Everest expedition and two years later was a member of Charles Evans' successful expedition to Kangchenjunga. He believed that an individual's discipline developed from sound training in outdoor activities.

Looking back at this period, it is easy to forget that outdoor education in any form was in its infancy. Almost every step was an experiment, with initiatives needing to be tried and tested then altered or discarded as was seen fit. The medium was developing very fast as centres opened elsewhere and local authorities began to see he value in using the outdoors. The first Mountain Centres Conference took place as early as October 962 - hosted by the Brenin. The instructional and omestic staff were praised for their outstanding ontribution to the success of the event. The ollowing year, on the recommendation of the Conference, an informal meeting of the Wardens of Mountain Centres was held at White Hall. Shortly after, they formed the Association of Wardens of Mountain Centres (AWMC). This led to today's Association of Heads of Outdoor Education Centres (AHOEC). But, while Plas y Brenin found itself with an ever-increasing level of competition, it was still the leader in terms of establishing what have become the linchpins in the teaching of mountaineering skills and their use in the development of individuals.

Plas y Brenin was also expanding physically. Within a couple of years of opening, the King George VI Foundation granted a further £10,000 to enable the CCPR to purchase the Cottage to provide staff accommodation, an equipment room and a field studies room. More work was also done on the main building to create lecture rooms, common rooms and a staff dining room. At this time, it was suggested that the Centre should buy Garth Farm to provide additional grazing for the trekking ponies but it was decided this would not be a sound investment. Also amongst the improvements considered, but dismissed, was the installation of central heating. Perhaps that became more of a priority when the Centre opted to open all year round and it was finally installed in 1965, paid for by a grant of £4,000 from the Ministry of Education. Despite the numerous alterations, the Welsh Office designated Plas y Brenin as a building of Special Architectural and Historical Interest the same year.

A visit from the Secretary of the King George VI Foundation, who described Plas y Brenin as the best enterprise the memorial funded, was instrumental in gaining an increase in the amount of money available. The release of more money enabled the Centre to buy the Annexe and incorporate it completely.

Looking at many outdoor centres today, it is hard to understand the Committee's reluctance to increase the number of students the Centre could accommodate by the simple addition of bunk beds. The debate continued for some time before a few were installed, increasing three bedded rooms to four. But then much that was commonplace forty or fifty years ago seems amusing or incredible now. With today's Health and

"

For many years, course charges were calculated by combining a daily rate with an instructional fee. There was a reduction for those schools, LEAs, training colleges and youth organisations who booked directly.

In 1956, charges were increased to:

	£ sd
Daily rate	*166*
Instruction fee (per day)	*36*

Specialist fees

rock climbing	*Task*
canoeing	*Task*
camping	*Task*
courses and fishing	*50*
field studies	*20*

Equipment hire (per week)

boots	*36*
anoraks	*26*
skis (inc. poles & boots)	*1.00*

A five day rock climbing course, including boot and anorak hire, would have worked out at approximately £6.00. In 2005, the equivalent five day course is £430.00.

"

Safety Regulations to be adhered to, the idea that experiments in the use of helmets for rock climbing courses only led to their subsequent introduction when they were deemed "successful" seems amazing. But not quite as amazing as the decision in 1962 that recent research into the harmful effects of smoking resulted in the Plas y Brenin shop discontinuing the sale of cigarettes - but only to those under 16! They remained available to everyone else.

Further expansion took place with the purchase of Bod Silin, a bothy in the Carneddau, which provided overnight accommodation for groups traversing from Ogwen to Aber. The building was sold to the CCPR by Lady Janet Douglas Pennant, who also permitted the Centre to run introductory canoe courses on the Afon Ogwen. By the mid-1970s, the cost of maintaining the bothy was becoming prohibitive and various solutions were tried, including providing free use of Bod Silin to Falmer School in exchange for work parties. It remained part of Plas y Brenin until 1976, when it was put up for sale because of the escalating maintenance cost. However, a sale was not actually completed until 1983.

When Gim Milton retired as Warden in 1960, John Jackson was his natural successor. Gim left to take up the post of Bursar at Oundle School. He retired to Northamptonshire where he died in February 2006.

By 1960, Plas y Brenin had moved into leadership training to enable others to use what they learned elsewhere. The earliest beneficiaries of this were those working for their Duke of Edinburgh's Award and a scheme was set up to combine this training with the development of Gold Award holders. Sir John Hunt gave permission for his expedition to Greenland's Staunings Alper to be the pilot for the scheme and he invited John Jackson to join him. While there was some opposition to the idea of taking youngsters on such a venture, this large expedition succeeded in making 14 first ascents and the first crossing on skis of the North Staunings via Col Major amongst other activities, including the mapping of hitherto virgin territory. Following the success of the trip, further Endeavour Expeditions took place, building the links between Plas y Brenin and not only the Duke of Edinburgh's

A BSAC sub aqua course in Llynnau Mymbyr in the early 1960s

ward Scheme but also the National Association of Youth Clubs (NAYC). Sir John Hunt also organised an xpedition on behalf of the NAYC, led by John Jackson, to the Pindus Mountains in Greece in 1963. In 1965, ere were over 100 Duke of Edinburgh's Gold Award applicants for places on an Endeavour Youth

John Jackson teaching navigation

Expedition to the Tatra Mountains in Czechoslovakia and Poland. Following a selection process, a dozen won places on the expedition, which was again led by Sir John Hunt, who was assisted by Roger Orgill. The links with what were then Iron Curtain countries continued, with Plas y Brenin arranging exchange visits with Russian, Polish and Czech mountaineers throughout the 1960s.

The early 1960s saw the abandonment of both pony trekking courses and sub-aqua activities. While these had been successful, both were going to require considerable investment and development if they were to continue in a way that would make them worthwhile, and that money was better spent on more traditional mountain activities.

This period also saw the advent of a long association with the Prison Service. Aidan Healey was in charge of training for Prison Officers and their development course was considered to be the elite of its kind. Over a period of about three months, Prison Officers were trained at four different venues, including both Bisham Abbey and Plas y Brenin. The range of subjects covered was very broad, already encompassing football, cricket and gymnastics, and the addition of outdoor skills enhanced it even further. The Plas y Brenin element lasted three weeks and included climbing, hillwalking, canoeing and overnight camps. These courses lasted until the early 1990s.

Away courses continued. The North Eastern region of the CCPR used Brenin staff to organise and run a course for 20 students in Borrowdale in 1962. And future courses at Plas y Brenin were being considered as it became obvious that formal qualifications were becoming necessary in mountaineering. With the successful take-up of Whitbread Bursary places, the potential value of a single term or one year course for teachers was being researched. The plan was that it would lead to the presentation of a "diploma" and the

Plas y Brenin The Snowdonia National Recreation Centre
Outdoor Activity Courses October 1984-April 1985

expectation was that the successful students would make a strong contribution to the continuing development of outdoor education. However, it was not possible to include this sort of course on the programme without the backing of the Ministry of Education.

Charles Burnup helped to launch a single term Outdoor Education course, which initially ran from January to March. Later, a second course was added in the autumn. These courses were extremely popular and the students included many from overseas. They gained great benefit from the continuity of instruction, which was designed to include winter work in the Cairngorms and Peak District. A week's placement at a LEA centre was included in the course. Charles Burnup went on to establish Kent County Council's outdoor centre in Llanberis and subsequently administered the Sports Council's Sport for All campaign.

John Jackson was one of the writers of 'Safety on Mountains', which was approved by the BMC, the Association of Scottish Climbing Clubs (ASCC) and the Scottish Council for Physical Recreation. The publication sold more than 17,000 copies within twelve months and continued to generate good sales afterwards. Increasingly, Plas y Brenin made a valuable contribution to the ever-growing mountaineering community with Jacko also working on a short film about rope handling and the CCPR producing 'Climb When You're Ready', both of them proving to be valuable resources in educating climbers.

Sir John Hunt retired as Chairman of the Management Committee in 1965 and Jack Longland took his place. Longland was also the Chairman of the CCPR's Outdoor Activity Advisory Committee. As a member of the Management Committee since its launch, it was a smooth transition.

The need for more facilities led to yet more construction - to extend the student lounge - and the leasing of Bryn Engan in 1965. Across the Afon Llugwy from the main buildings, it provided useful staff accommodation as the Centre continued to grow. The lease was only for 21 years but, by 1983, Plas y Brenin had bought the freehold enabling its use to continue uninterrupted.

In 1965, the Mountain Rescue Committee (MRC) invited Plas y Brenin to become a Mountain Rescue Post. Rescue teams were the "self-help" service provided by mountaineers for their fellows and were becoming more organised as the numbers taking to the hills increased. Around the time of the establishment of the Rescue Post, teams were coming into being in both Llanberis and the Ogwen Valley. The BMC and MRC helped with the organisation of rescue courses for team members and staff from centres and a mountain rescue conference was held at Plas y Brenin in December 1966. When Derek Mayes joined the instructional staff in November of that year, his dog Rikki arrived with him. She subsequently completed her search dog training and was part of Centre life until her untimely death in a road accident a few years later. Derek fulfilled a number of roles over the years as he remained at Plas y Brenin until 1997, by which time he had worked for every head of Centre bar Gim Milton.

In 1967, Plas y Brenin suffered a financial blow when an epidemic of foot and mouth disease broke out. The Farmers' Union requested a curtailment of all movement and courses had to be restricted to the Centre

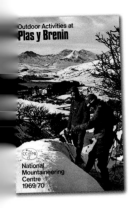

Outdoor Activities at
Plas y Brenin

National Mountaineering Centre 1969/70

grounds. John Jackson had no option but to offer students who had already booked a choice between a restricted programme or a refund. But even the restricted programme, which ran for a month from mid-November, could not save Plas y Brenin from complete closure as a result of the epidemic. On 6 December 1967 Plas y Brenin closed its doors and they did not reopen until 17 February 1968. The net loss of income - £3,150 - was heavy. Fortunately, bookings had been maintained at a high level with a continuing increase in specialist and leadership training courses. It was estimated that, without the foot and mouth losses, Centre occupancy would have been as high as 96% for that administrative year.

Staffing levels were no longer sufficient for the number of courses run at Plas y Brenin and, in 1968, it was decided to increase the instructional staff by one. Some title changes also came into being with the Warden becoming the Director and his Deputy becoming the Chief Instructor and Deputy Director. The Director was granted the authority to employ temporary instructors where necessary and also to open up the Centre to non-residential courses. As a result, revenue was bolstered by the introduction of day courses and the use of some facilities - notably the artificial ski slope - by the local community. The scheme extended to the training pool, weight drop machine and the cross country ski track and there was a gradual widening in use of the facilities.

By the time Plas y Brenin became the National Mountaineering Centre in 1968 it was a change in name only. It had taken just 13 years to fix the Centre very firmly in the psyche of a United Kingdom that was going through a rapid period of change in almost every respect. "The Brenin" was known to the general public as well as to those within the close knit circle of mountaineering.

A new era arrived in outdoor education with the expansion of National Governing Body (NGB) Awards.

A £10,000 improvement to the skiing facilities brought the support of the National Ski Federation of Great Britain and, with it, Instructor and Advanced Artificial Ski courses. In March 1969, the Centre was

66 ————

Opposition to the introduction of bunk beds, where concerns were that room size:

"may not be adequate for the maintenance of the standards of civilised and civilising residence that the CCPR has always set out to maintain at its Centres. Quite apart from the wardrobe and drawer space required, it would not seem possible to give each resident a chair on which to put his clothes at night in such conditions."

Management Committee Minutes March 1959

———— 99

John Jackson

host to the first Welsh Ski Championships and spectator sports had arrived at Plas y Brenin. By 1970, the British biathlon cross-country ski team was making use of the facilities for a training week.

The Centre was also offering evening starter classes in skiing for local children. While the take up amongst instructors' children was inevitably high - not just those actually working at the Brenin, but from other centres too - many others took advantage of the opportunity to receive a sound grounding from highly qualified staff. Within a very short time, junior members of the North Wales Dragons Ski Club were taking part in race training at Alpbach in Austria and competing at a national level. Several made the move to senior level including Robin Jackson, Jacko's son, who competed for Britain in the Europa Cup and was part of the squad from which the 1976 British Winter Olympic ski team was drawn.

In mountaineering, the awards were being developed from scratch. Mountain guiding had been very much an ad hoc business prior to the establishment of the BMC. Guiding through a mountainous area or up a specific peak had been done on reputation alone, although as early as 1861 Capel Curig was home to Robin Hughes whose occupation was "Guide to the Snowdonia Hills". By 1950, Mountain Guide was a recognised qualification and George "Scotty" Dwyer was the first holder of the award in North Wales. The qualification was divided into sections - Mountain Guide and Rock Climbing Guide, with the ASCC offering an additional part for working in Scotland. Since the scheme was set up and run by the BMC, the holders were known as BMC Guides. Initially, carnets were awarded for a limited three year period and holders had to be re-tested.

In its early days, the Guides' carnet could have been regarded as something of an award for the old boy network, as it was gained by proving practical competence to the satisfaction of the applicant's peers. During the 1960s, however, as the number of aspirants increased, more stringent testing was developed, which involved demonstrating skills over extended periods. It gradually became the elite qualification known today although many Guides still worked in centres rather than independently.

By 1975, the Association of British Mountain Guides (ABMG) had been established and the Guides became autonomous, although both the BMC and the Mountaineering Council of Scotland (MCofS) were represented on their committee. It was obvious that steps needed to be taken to ensure that British Guides could legally work abroad but the British carnet was not recognised elsewhere. However, initial attempts to gain international recognition through membership of the Union Internationale des Associations des Guides de Montagne (UIAGM) were unsuccessful. It was not until 1977 that the application was accepted and then conditions were applied. The training and assessment had to be expanded and Alpine elements - including skiing - were introduced. It has continued to expand, becoming an all encompassing qualification that can be used across the globe.

Numbers remained low - it took nearly 50 years for the Guides to reach their 100th carnet. Plas y Brenin and Glenmore Lodge have never had difficulty retaining Guides - at the end of 2005 there are 11 amongst the Brenin's permanent staff. But many other carnet holders have moved increasingly to freelance work over the last 20 years as other qualifications have been introduced to reflect the needs of centres. However, for the National Centres, the benefits of retaining a high proportion of Guides are seen in the depth of experience they bring. Plas y Brenin can run climbing, mountaineering and ski-mountaineering courses in the Alps and further field without the need to buy in staff knowing that, even if they did so, the calibre would be no higher.

The Mountain Training Board, which became the Mountain Leader Training Board (MLTB) and later split into separate Boards for the UK, Scotland, Wales and England, was set up in 1964. Its original remit was the creation and administration of a certificate of competence in leadership of mountain activities. Inevitably, the links with Plas y Brenin were strong because many of the committee were also involved with the national centre. Jack Longland was the first Chairman, John Jackson represented the CCPR and Sir John Hunt was an independent member of the Mountain Training Board.

Creating the Mountain Leadership Certificate (MLC) qualification from scratch and ensuring that it fulfilled the needs demanded of it took some time. Such was the thought that went into it, that the current logbook system with a requirement for an Introductory and an Assessment course and the maintenance of a log book remains little changed from its accreditation in 1964 although its name has changed to the Mountain Leader (ML) Award (Summer). MLC courses were not restricted to Plas y Brenin, and White Hall, Brathay Hall and the Outward Bound Mountain Schools were all authorised to conduct both training and assessment. As the take-up grew and the scheme expanded, more centres were authorised to provide training courses although assessment was still restricted to the original group.

In Scotland, the requirements were amended to take account of the need for additional snow and ice skills and an extra Scottish Winter tier was added to accommodate that.

Having established the scheme, it was essential that people started to use it. The Brenin's links with many organisations helped to promote it and also ensured that their own MLC courses were well attended. The main problem initially was that colleges of education were not selecting candidates carefully enough and a number of failures were down to little more than lack of planning and intensity during the assessment phase.

With those wanting to lead groups in the mountains now accredited, the additional need for a qualification for instructors came to the forefront. The Association of Wardens of Mountain Centres (AWMC) proposed the implementation of a scheme of certification but progress was stalled when it was decided that one qualification, rather than different schemes, was necessary. As a result, an umbrella committee comprising the English, Welsh and Scottish Training Boards, the BMC, the Mountaineering Association and the AWMC drew up the proposals for implementing a single qualification with the necessary courses being run by Plas y Brenin and Glenmore Lodge. This produced the Mountain Instructor's (Professional) Certificate and the Mountain Instructor's (Advanced) Certificate - the MIC - and accreditation took place in 1969. It was agreed that the scheme should be administered by the Mountain Training Board and it continued to be so after administration of the MLTB came under the BMC's remit in 1972.

At Plas y Brenin, the first ski award courses were quickly followed by the first Mountain Instructor's Certificate (MIC) course in January 1969, the second running as early as March of the same year. In 1970 John Jackson - with Kim Meldrum, the Principal of White Hall - ran an MIC course for 42 candidates. Ten gained their MIC and one the Advanced Certificate. An overflow of 40 candidates had to attend a course at Glenmore Lodge. Over the years the scheme has developed but the importance of the qualification remains unchanged. During the first two decades of the MIC, those gaining it averaged fewer than 10 per year and, even in 2005, the number is scarcely double that.

After the initial rush, while the number of MIC candidates remained relatively small for some years, those

The first course for the disabled :

"The course was an overwhelming success and the main lesson learned was plain : as long as there were no medical reasons to the contrary, experienced instructors could introduce a great many physically handicapped people to a large range of outdoor pursuits."

"That course at Plas y Brenin symbolised all I had hoped for; the participants had a taste of what I had had for many years from climbing. No special organisation had been set up, for this was a system by which disabled people could be integrated into ordinary centres."

Norman Croucher

High Hopes, pp 134 and 135, pb Hodder & Stoughton 1976

wishing to gain the MLC were more plentiful, but there was still some concern that they were not all up to the standard required. The method of booking courses made it difficult for Plas y Brenin staff to help students to prepare adequately and by the early 1970s it was suggested that course bookings should be made directly with Plas y Brenin.

Yet again, Plas y Brenin was undergoing physical changes too. By the summer of 1971 the bar had been completed. Throughout changes over the years, it has remained a focal point of the social character of the Brenin. Three years later, Glyder Cottage was altered to make room for new development and, in 1976, the ground floor of Bryn Engan was altered to enable it to be used as temporary bunkhouse accommodation.

The Disabled Living Foundation started an investigation into outdoor facilities for the disabled in 1973. The following year, they produced a Directory of Outdoor Activities for Disabled People. It was to herald the growth of non-competitive activities in that field. Norman Croucher, who had become known for his mountaineering activities following the loss of both his legs, helped Plas y Brenin to pioneer a course for the disabled, the first of which ran in June 1975. Initially accommodation was provided in the main building but, later, the temporary bunkhouse in Bryn Engan enabled the provision of suitable accommodation for the students. John Jackson's view was that "such courses are not at all too difficult or too dangerous or too much of a problem". Not only did the students include those with a wide range of physical handicaps but the activities included were also diverse. Any argument that the disabled can only follow a particular activity if they happen to have participated prior to becoming disabled was totally disproved. One simple rule applied - that every participant "should be dealt with individually. In outdoor pursuits a handicap should not be ignored, but properly taken into account". Of course, the principle that each student is treated as an individual applies equally to everyone and has always been fundamentally important in outdoor education.

Norman then joined the Management Committee and provided valuable input during his time as a member. In 1978, Norman produced a booklet based mainly on his experiences at Plas y Brenin - 'Here to Stay: Disabled People in Outdoor Centres'. While the course for the physically disabled was declared an unqualified success, one for mentally disabled students was not as satisfactory and the venture was not repeated after it was decided that Plas y Brenin was not a suitable environment.

The early 1970s saw a rapid increase in the number of training courses offered. In 1973, a total of 68 MLC

Minister for Sport Denis Howell during Sports Council Members' visit to North Wales 1969. Left to right front row- John Jackson, Derek Mayes, Denis Howell and Ray Greenall. Sir Jack Longland, chair of PYB Management group centre rear and Roger Orgill rear left.

This was the occasion when Denis Howell , following a great lunch at the Centre, famously announced that before his next visit he wished to see the creation of an enlarged lecture room and ski slope, a heated canoe training pool and a licensed bar. It was October and Sports Council was to fund this and account for it by March end the following year. Ski slope enlargement was carried out by staff and other work by outside contractors

courses - 43 Introductory and 25 Assessment - were held. As more and more teachers and youth workers applied for the qualification, Plas y Brenin was in danger of being overwhelmed by its own success in the field of training. The decision was made to expand the number of other centres permitted to run MLC courses, while the MIC remained the exclusive territory of the Brenin, Glenmore Lodge and Tollymore in Ireland. A large number of the providers that subsequently took on the task of ML training and assessment were LEA run. The need for the change was emphasised as the number of places required continued to increase. By 1990, nearly 2000 candidates were registering for the ML Award each year.

By the mid-1970s, Plas y Brenin needed to revise its programme to enable more rock climbing courses to be introduced with a consequent reduction in MLC courses. By 1974, the Centre had halved its number of ML courses, while still taking 25% of all that ran.

The need for this level of qualification was justified by the large number of youngsters experiencing some sort of introduction to hills and mountains through schools, youth clubs and similar organisations, who subsequently went on to take their skills to a higher level. As the demand for outdoor education continued to grow apace, the instructors of the future were developing through their teachers' and leaders' love of the medium and desire to pass on that interest to new generations. Many of the 21st century's instructors will have taken their first steps along their career path under the guidance of an MLC holder trained through, or as a result, of Plas y Brenin's involvement with the scheme from its earliest days.

In 1972 the Welsh Wool shop gave way to what is now the Plas y Brenin Equipment Store

This was entirely in line with John Jackson's approach during his tenure as Director of the Centre. He firmly believed that it was essential not to separate out the sundry parts of mountain activities. Over recent years, the fractures between the different aspects of the activities have shown more visibly, dividing to even include those who never venture beyond the confines of an indoor climbing wall. But Jackson consistently adhered to his view that "rock climbing should not become divorced from mountaineering, but always be seen in the context as part of the mountaineer's skill."

Plas y Brenin expanded when the tenancies of both the British Legion and the Welsh Wool Shop came to an end. The British Legion room was converted to a lecture room. It had been decided that, when the Lease for the Welsh Wool Shop ended in August 1971, it would not be renewed but Mr and Mrs Davies, the tenants, announced their intention to retire in early 1972 so a six month extension was granted and the shop then closed its doors for the last time. By then, their daughter had established a similar business in Betws y Coed - Anna Davies - that continues to thrive.

The Sports Council hoped to take on the administration of the Whitbread Sports Fund when it established the Sports Council Trust, a charitable body. It had been decided that the Sports Council could not own property and all the National Recreation Centres were affected by the change although, in reality, it made little difference. Ownership of Plas y Brenin was transferred to the new Trust but the Management Committee and Terms of Reference for the Centre remained unaltered.

It was an opportunity for some regrading and restructuring amongst the instructional staff and funding could now come via the Trust's Fund when capital expenditure for equipment was necessary. The role of Senior nstructor was introduced and it was hoped to appoint someone from among the existing staff. Derek Mayes vas appointed to the post. He ranked immediately below the Chief Instructor and Deputy Director. To take ccount of the increasing number of courses and students, it was agreed that two or three additional ermanent instructors would be employed.

The instructors' equipment allowance was increased from £30 to £40 per annum and temporary instructors' wages were doubled to £20. The sum of £350 was set aside for in-service training for staff and several took advantage of opportunities to work elsewhere in the world for short periods, returning with their own skills and motivation enhanced.

Despite these changes, there were times when it was difficult to get a broad field of suitable candidates when posts came vacant and Jacko believed that this was, at least in part, due to the change in leave allocation. It had been set at four weeks, which was off-putting for applicants who were currently working in schools or colleges and also for many who wanted to participate in expeditions. While that experience was an essential part of maintaining skills, it was impossible to take the necessary amount of time off except where special permission had been granted.

In 1974, the Management Committee met with the staff to fend off rumours that the Sports Council was about to sell Plas y Brenin. They were reassured that the only anticipated change was a slight shift from the Centre's early direction - where its links with mainstream education were strongest - to its current role as a centre in pursuit of excellence in special sports and in the training of leaders and coaches. The aim was to make the National Recreation Centres "brand leaders" in their fields.

Change was ahead at the time of Jacko's departure in 1975, but he had driven Plas y Brenin forward to a place of unrivalled standing in its field. Gone were the days when athletics might have had to be considered if there was insufficient demand for mountaineering and the pony trekking and underwater swimming were distant memories. Even the softer courses - local myth and legend - had been replaced by the more challenging Expedition Photography, Orienteering and Mountain Structure and Life. But it was the unprecedented level of training that enabled Plas y Brenin to reach the point where it was finally able to offer a single term course in outdoor education for qualified teachers, under the auspices of the Department of Education and Science in 1971.

After he left Plas y Brenin, John Jackson effectively retired, fulfilling an ambition to drive to India climbing, skiing and exploring along the way. But it was not long before he was asked to once again put his skills to good use, becoming a consultant during the establishment of Plas Menai. He went on to become first Principal of the newly opened Centre - the National Outdoor Centre for Wales. Even after he retired again - for good this time - he continued to introduce people to the outdoors. Jacko ran treks to the Himalaya, South America and Galapagos Islands as well as mountaineering and skiing trips to the Alps. Even into his 80s, he was able to enjoy his beloved mountains in good company, his passion undimmed. After playing such a significant role in the development of Plas y Brenin and in outdoor education and training generally, John Jackson died in July 2005.

A typical day on a Plas y Brenin Scottish Winter Mountaineering course.

The Activities

The 50th Anniversary Edition of the Plas y Brenin brochure runs to over 50 pages and the courses offered range from an Orienteering Family Funfest with barbecue to an ascent of Mont Blanc.

As a national mountaineering centre the focus has always been on mountain activities but that remit can be broadly interpreted. Many of the activities that are routinely expected at an outdoor centre in the 21st century were unimaginable by all but the most farsighted 50 years ago. Obviously, rock climbing and the broader spectrum of mountaineering were catered for and canoeing was available from the start. But fly-fishing and local history sat easily alongside the more physical activities in the 1950s and it was not until 1979 that angling reached a point where it was no longer considered viable. It was ironic that, within a few years, disputes between canoeists and anglers were leading to problems not just for Plas y Brenin, but for many other centres.

The purpose of many of these softer courses was, perhaps, to bring more people into the hills and a gentler introduction could achieve a level of interest that may or may not develop. Pony trekking was extremely popular elsewhere although it might not have been added to the Brenin's course list had Gim Milton not been such a keen horseman himself. In retrospect, it must have been an especially good way to introduce girls to the mountain environment. At the time it was growing in popularity and would have encouraged them to participate more in the outdoors.

Although Outward Bound was expanding rapidly, it still had no facility specifically for female courses. Consequently, in its early years, Plas y Brenin ran their courses for girls, including the ourse that launched the Centre.

Fittingly, the final girls' Outward Bound course was also memorable as it ran in tandem with a Royal Military Academy Sandhurst cadet exercise. The girls, much rehearsed, acted as agents in enemy territory. The cadets were undoubtedly dismayed to discover their contact was a teenage girl, but she fulfilled her duty by leading them safely over the Glyders to the Ogwen Valley. The girls also provided

canoe safety support for the cadets.

By the 1960s, Outward Bound had invested in Rhowniar, near Tywyn in Meirionydd. Although in close proximity to the first Outward Bound school at Aberdyfi and very much part of Outward Bound Wales, Rhowniar was the "girls' school" and the courses moved from the Brenin. In time Rhowniar and Aberdovey both became co-educational.

Almost from the day it opened, Plas y Brenin offered training courses to teach others to introduce people to the hills. Whether it was courses for teachers (later followed by the MLC which opened the hills to many school groups) or courses and expeditions for young people like the participants on the early Duke of Edinburgh's Award Scheme, the effect was to multiply those who accessed the mountains. By the end of the 1960s, the MIC and MLC were developing rapidly and the take up, especially of the latter, was increasing all the time. These were followed by other awards as they were introduced - the SPA, Walking Group Leader Award (WGL), International Mountain Leader Award (IML) and Guide courses. While any centre authorised to provide the ML award may also run WGL courses, only Plas y Brenin and Glenmore Lodge currently offer the IML. This award, which grew out of the European Mountain Leader Award, provides a qualification enabling leaders to work in all areas that are neither glaciated nor require climbing and Alpinism techniques.

Even today, when overall participation numbers have escalated, the importance of training at all levels cannot be emphasised enough. Without qualified instructors and Guides the whole outdoor education business would stall. Increasingly, the need for physical recreation, particularly for youngsters, is being recognised and the opportunities offered by the countryside as a whole should not be underestimated. Every year since it opened, Plas y Brenin has been responsible for placing in the wider community skilled exponents of mountain activities who operate with competence and confidence and are able to credibly spread the gospel.

Sitting comfortably around the training courses were Plas y Brenin's original Basic Course, which provided an introduction to map reading, canoeing, rock climbing, mountain camping and survival. The last night was always an overnight camp, putting the skills learned to good use.

Canoeing was quickly expanding. The Centre initially had just two canoes - one double and one single lathe and canvas PBK to be shared between 10 students - and Roger Orgill built more to increase the fleet to a dozen. By 1959, the first fibreglass canoes had been purchased and 10 years later, a stock of C1s and C2s arrived.

At the time Plas y Breni opened, Roger Orgill wa already an excellent canoei although he was more tha capable of instructing in ever branch of the activitie offered. Tim Aron, a membe of the Alpine Club, had arrive as an expert mountaineer an skier but he soon learned t canoe. It was to be expected that the mountaineering and climbing staff at Plas y Brenin would be the highest quality

Outward Bound student under instruction in canoe building with Roger Orgill.

available, something the Centre has always prided itself on, and over the years its water-based activities brought to Plas y Brenin Coaches of superb calibre. Some of the best known names in canoeing - including Derek Mayes, Jim Hargreaves, Nigel Timmins, Ray Rowe, Peter Midwood, Franco Ferrero and Loel Collins - were prominent members of Plas y Brenin staff. By the mid-1990s canoeing was in decline at the Centre, due in part to the opening of Plas Menai, but there has since been a rapid rise in the courses offered, with an almost threefold increase since 1995. Even when the frequency of courses was decreasing, Plas y Brenin retained top level coaches, which enabled the resurgence in the activity to be accomplished when it came about.

It was natural that Plas y Brenin would offer British Canoe Union courses at all levels in tandem with their mountaineering qualifications. Plas y Brenin has been at the forefront of delivering the BCU Level 5

Martin Chester and head of Canoeing Loel Collins enjoying some leisure time.

oaching Award, although they have recently supported Glenmore Lodge staff enabling them to once again provide the course. In 2005, there were eight BCU Level 5 Coaches working at Plas y Brenin.

Within a decade of opening, Plas y Brenin had installed a dry ski slope that was quickly utilised by the National Ski Federation of Great Britain for courses, training and competition. The slope has been developed over the years, lengthened and widened and with the addition of a tow. It is an asset that has brought consistent revenue to Plas y Brenin being used for everything from taster days to specialist training. Mike Keating's work as Ski Facilities Officer in the late 1970s and into the 1980s was recognised as having a great impact "of national significance" on the development of skiing at Plas y Brenin. So it is not surprising that several British ski champions have either learned to ski or honed their skills at the Centre and that it is home to the North Wales Dragons Ski Club.

The British Ski Club for the disabled continue to meet each month at Plas y Brenin.

For many years there was also a cross country ski trail on the other side of the river where telemark training could take place. It was only the increase in orienteering that caused this facility to fall out of use as the space was needed.

1975 saw the introduction of the pilot course for the disabled. It is perhaps best described in Outdoor Pursuits for Disabled People by Norman Croucher, who was so instrumental in the introduction of the courses and helped enormously with the development of outdoor education for the disabled, as well as changing the public's perceptions of what disability actually meant.

"Nearly 20 physically handicapped people attended . . . the majority were within the 14 to 18 year age bracket but some older handicapped individuals were there as instructors. Handicaps included cerebral palsy, polio, spina bifida, paraplegia (T9 complete), rheumatoid arthritis, terratoma of spine, multiple sclerosis (all wheelchair users) and several other handicaps which did not prevent walking. A broad range of activities including ski-bobbing, dry-slope skiing, snorkelling, sailing, canoeing, tobogganing, hillwalking, angling, rowing and climbing were tackled in what proved to be a very enjoyable week."

This course was rapidly followed up with a subsequent one including the visually impaired and a third designed specifically to introduce those visiting staff familiar with disabilities to outdoor activities and vice versa. So Plas y Brenin continued to build on its reputation for training the trainers.

Over time, specialist courses have been seen as less necessary and many of the Brenin's courses are equally accessible, particularly canoeing and kayaking. The refurbishment of the student

Bill March became Dircetor in the mid 1970's

accommodation at the Centre has included the creation of sever rooms that provide the facilities required - ground floor acces wider doors, spacious rooms and en suite showers. Making th: necessary adaptations in buildings that are both old and protecte can be difficult but clever use of the available space has enable Plas y Brenin to become much more user-friendly even fo wheelchair users.

By the mid-1970s, when Bill March became Director of Plas Brenin, the range of courses offered had settled into one that me the needs of customers while actively contributing to the wide field of the mountaineering world. As well as rock climbing mountaineering and the training courses for NGB awards, there was the opportunity to look at Mountain Structure and Life or learn the art of Expedition Photography. Ski courses were expanding and Orienteering had become a regular fixture on the calendar.

Support from the British Orienteering Federation (BOF) brought training courses to Plas y Brenin and saw the preparation of new maps. By 1979 it was obvious that a full time orienteering instructor was necessary to cope with the demands of this growing activity. In 1983, the Centre's reputation was enhanced when the BOF nominated Plas y Brenin as a National Centre for Coaching. With Martin Bagness, the national Champion, working at Plas y Brenin it was inevitable that growth would escalate at this time. Isabel Inglis was also very active in promoting orienteering and a series of events for children attracted more than 150 and led to the setting up of a local orienteering club. Later, Anne Salisbury continued the promotion, including the children's evening events. In 2005, Malcolm Campbell, an ex-Plas y Brenin instructor, re-mapped the area bringing the Centre up to date.

First Aid and Search and Survival courses helped the increasing number of people taking to the hills to do so in greater safety. Specialist courses for mountain rescue teams often gave those who operated in the lower ranges their first experience with the aircraft that were becoming an essential part of the service in regions like Snowdonia. Over the years, this was one area where the courses offered by Plas y Brenin diminished, as the MRC expanded to enable many teams to self-train. Now, only the highly skilled Scottish Winter training is included in the Brenin's calendar.

A valid first aid certificate is a requirement for most NGB instructional awards so Plas y Brenin always offers the appropriate courses. The earliest specialised first aid course specifically for mountaineers was established by Dr Ieuan Jones when he was Senior Casualty Consultant at Bangor and Anglesey Hospital and then at its replacement, Ysbyty Gwynedd. The course was bought in as a package run by trained instructors at a variety of venues across the UK, including Plas y Brenin. In recent years, all the first aid courses have been under the authority of Rescue Emergency Care (REC). With several different levels of course offered - including one for trainers - every aspect of providing emergency care in the mountains and on water is covered. This includes both the Advanced and High Altitude REC Certificates.

as y Brenin's earliest "away" course was the Welsh river canoeing trip run by Gim Milton and Roger Orgill. The Duke of Edinburgh's Award Scheme training expeditions to Greenland and Greece took students further afield but this was just the beginning. The Centre widened its horizons even further with the introduction of regular Alpine courses and more Scottish Winter work. Throughout the 1980s, more new opportunities presented themselves - Kenyan Exploration, Alpine Canoeing and Spanish Rock courses were taken up with enthusiasm.

Mike (Twid) Turner climbing on the Hotrock' course in Spain.

It was necessary that some of the courses taking students abroad were entirely self-financing. The first trip to Mount Kenya was an outstanding success with all but one of the party reaching the summit by various routes. A last minute glitch with the flights meant that the course had to carry a loss of £185 but this was not sufficient for future courses to be jeopardised. The possibility of further away courses was explored - orienteering in Sweden, canoeing in Norway and ski-mountaineering in Alaska.

For many years Plas y Brenin has provided opportunities for outdoor enthusiasts to develop their skills as outdoor instructors and teachers as voluntary instructors and, in recent years, as trainee instructors. The newest initiative sees the Centre offer the Fast Track Instructor Scheme. Aimed at those who are serious about their desire to work in outdoor education, this 15 week course provides a wealth of practical experience combined with the opportunity to gain a range of mountaineering, paddling and orienteering qualifications together with First Aid and Off Site Safety Management Certificates. Successfully completing a course like this at Plas y Brenin enhances the reputation of any new instructor and the take-up has shown the continuing upward trend in this field with six students in 2004, 12 in 2005 and 16 registered for 2006. For those passing through this scheme, it has proved to be an effective way of gaining work in the outdoor field.

Scottish Winter Mountaineering with Plas y Brenin

Making the most of early season Winter conditions in Scotland.

From the mid-1980s, Plas y Brenin ran a seve[n]
week module in Countryside Management for t[he]
University College of North Wales in Bang[or]
Some initial concerns about the role the Cent[re]
could play in this field were dispelled and th[e]
course quickly developed. It covered several are[as]
and included its own away sections, making fu[ll]
use of the Snowdonia environment to show th[e]
practicalities of the subject. As well as bas[ic]
mountaincraft, including solo bivouacs, studen[ts]
spent a week on Ynys Enlli. They studied th[e]
traditional activites - rock climbing, winte[r]
mountaineering and sea kayaking but combine[d]
them with photography, poetry , creative writin[g]
and estate management.

Those looking for a specialised area of training, bu[t]
not necessarily resulting in a NGB Award, are als[o]
catered for. Courses for Duke of Edinburgh'[s]
Award leaders continue Plas y Brenin's long
association with a scheme that had its advent at the
same time and has brought many to awareness of
the opportunities offered by the hills through its
expedition section. Similarly, the Scouts benefit
from subsidised leadership courses, with particular
emphasis on helping them to become "Scout Assessors" in the outdoors.

There has never been a need to arrive with a wealth of experience for Plas y Brenin's introductory courses.
Absolute beginners can gain as much from the five day Rambling in Snowdonia course currently offered as
an experienced ski mountaineer will from the same length of time spent Alpine Ski Touring. Many use Plas
y Brenin courses to build their confidence and experience in a range of activities while also participating
independently at other times. For those seeking a career in outdoor education, the NGB Awards - both
training and assessment - are always on offer with many additional opportunities to add to them either by
concentrating on a weakness such as navigation or first aid or by improving knowledge in areas like
avalanche awareness or white water safety and rescue.

For this 50th anniversary year, Plas y Brenin has created a
range of special courses covering a variety of activities in a
number of places. From the orienteering absolute beginner
to the experienced climber, skier or paddler there is
something just a little unusual on offer. Enthusiasm for
some of these special courses has been strong enough for
them to be included in future years. In addition, and in

Alltshellach, Plas y Brenin's base in Scotland since 1994

Mountain Bike Leader courses make a welcome addition to the programme in 2005

keeping with its part in the community of Capel Curig and its surrounding area, one-day outdoor skills workshops have been offered throughout the anniversary year. Heavily subsidised, the days are specifically geared towards local youngsters, introducing them to their own environment and hopefully triggering a lifelong interest.

The anniversary courses for local youngsters builds on the existing activities offered through the youth club structure. While these are not set events, it is not unusual for Plas y Brenin to host youth clubs up to three evenings a week in summer, offering free tuition to 8-16 year olds in a variety of fields.

Its 51st year of operation will bring new developments. Plas y Brenin's winter courses have most recently been run from Alltshellach, originally built as a country residence for the Bishop of Argyll. Situated on the shores of Loch Leven, Alltshellach is ideally situated for both Glencoe and Ben Nevis and puts many other areas within easy access. For nine weeks each winter, Plas y Brenin has exclusive use of the house and its staff. In 2006, mountain walking, scrambling, mountaineering and climbing courses in May and June based at Alltshellach have been added to the programme.

Also, for the first time, mountain biking qualifications are included with both the Trail Cycle Leader and the Mountain Bike Leader Training and Assessment levels of the Scottish Mountain Bike Leader Award scheme on offer.

It can safely be said that Plas y Brenin has never failed to meet its remit. Its success is such that the Centre now runs near maximum capacity; 2005 saw 5,500 residential students on courses with over 50,000 session visitors. With a high level of satisfaction amongst students Plas y Brenin is undoubtedly worthy of its prestigious standing in the outdoor world with a range of activities unmatched elsewhere. With its high calibre staff, broad range of mountain related activities, focus and sense of purpose there is no doubt that Plas y Brenin is internationally recognised as a centre of excellence.

Llynnau Mymbyr and the Snowdon Horseshoe in the Background - an unrivalled location for the National Mountain Centre

A Centre of Excellence

Following John Jackson's departure, 1976 ushered in a new era when Bill March was appointed Director, having impressed the Sports Council with his development plans for Plas y Brenin. His links with the Centre went back to his own early career, when he had worked as a VI in the mid-1960s.

Even under new leadership, the restructuring continued at Plas y Brenin and Bill's title was altered to Principal. He was not averse to change and brought in a number of staff initiatives in an effort to drive Plas y Brenin forward. In 1969, the permanent instructors had been on open ended contracts rather than the three year renewable ones that had existed for such a long time. A new condition had been imposed - that over the age of 50 the contract became short term (with a maximum renewal period of three years) although it would be possible to renew more than once. In an effort to prevent stagnation, Bill oversaw the introduction of the five year contract, which was not welcomed initially but led to a through-flow of high quality instructional staff, each bringing their individual talents along with fresh ideas.

The domestic and administrative staff had been moved onto the NJC salary scale and conditions in 1974. And now, at the same time that contracts were reviewed, the instructors were also given the option of moving to the Civil Service Instructors' Salary scale or remaining on their current Administrative grades.

Ever since Plas y Brenin opened, problems had arisen with members of staff in posts requiring them to be ingle wanting to marry. This had, at times, put a great strain on the staff accommodation and it had only been through an extensive programme of redevelopment that the Centre was able to ensure that everyone who was required to live in - or chose to - was able to do so. By the 1970s staff who chose to live out received an allowance of £250 pa to help with their additional expenses. Eventually even the senior staff were permitted to live out provided they fulfilled duty obligations. To assist them, a duty bedroom was set aside for the occasions they needed to stay overnight at the Brenin. Partly because of the space it created, Bill moved permanent staff off-site where possible and encouraged only those on short term contracts to remain in staff accommodation.

Although there had always been away courses it was March who expanded the number included in the Centre's programme, establishing some as annual events. The Scottish Winter Climbing course, which remains on the programme to this day, was formalised and it was hoped it would create better connections with Glenmore Lodge. That liaison did not develop in the way that Bill March had hoped but the course was a success. He also introduced the Alpine Climbing course, made possible by the quality of instructors working at or available to Plas y Brenin. His vision continued the advance of the Centre as a market leader as others followed where Plas y Brenin led, but few could compete with the opportunities presented by Plas y Brenin's trips abroad.

An Open Day was held and was very well attended. The Centre's facilities remained an asset for the local community. Capel Curig children were taught to swim in the training pool and skiing continued to develop. Within a very short space of time, two television production companies used Plas y Brenin to film location scenes. Not only did this bring in a fee but the Centre was seen onscreen later. Even relatively small events like these could help to promote Plas y Brenin positively. Any revenue generated outside the actual courses run by Plas y Brenin was welcome and Bill March proposed that staff should undertake a lecture programme throughout the country that would not only produce some income but would help with promotion.

The timing was perfect. In 1975 a British expedition had made the first ascent of Everest by the difficult South-West Face route, with Dougal Haston and Doug Scott becoming the first Britons to reach

Recollections of a course:

In 1977, I was a student on Plas y Brenin's first Alpine White Water course. We were a group of about eight students led by Jim Hargreaves.

We started with a preparatory weekend in mid-March, based at PyB and paddling both days on the Serpent's Tail at Llangollen.

On 4 June we assembled at the Brenin to pack for the two week course - all food, tents and equipment were provided as part of the course. We travelled by minibus to a campsite near Durance, just south of Briançon, in the Dauphinée region of France.

During the course we paddled stretches of the Durance, the Gironde, the Guissane, the Clarée and the Guil. There was no English guide book available in those days and we had to rely on local information that Jim obtained from a local paddler. Because he was the fishmonger - Le Poissonier - we nicknamed him The Poisoner. The spring melt meant that water levels were very high and the Durance's Rabioux rapid was washed out. On the way home we visited the artificial slalom course at Vichy.

Di Airey 2005

Plas y Brenin
National
Mountaineering
Centre

PROGRAMME
October 1974 - December 1975

the summit. This expedition had received a great deal of media coverage including tv and radio reports. While the public had had the opportunity to see climbers in action over the previou decade with a few ascents televised live, this was the first majo British expedition to benefit from modern technology. The team's return to the UK was followed by a successful lecture tour. Plas y Brenin was able to take advantage of this by running promotional stalls at a number of the Everest lecture venues and then carried out its own lecture programme while interest in mountaineering was raised.

The mountain rescue training offered by Plas y Brenin was at its height in the 1970s, and many teams took advantage of the courses on offer. Plas y Brenin was able to include helicopter training, thanks to the proximity of RAF Valley on Anglesey. Each course would have one or two days set aside for students to be flown in to perform exercises in tricky locations. At that time Wessex helicopters were in use and, while working with the aircraft was routine for some mountain rescue teams - including the local Ogwen Valley and Llanberis ones - for many attendees it was a rare opportunity to learn the skills involved before they might have to be put into use in a "live" situation.

Bill March remained in post a very short time - just 18 months - but made his mark very clearly with results that may be seen to this day. His enthusiasm was infectious and he had a reputation for actively encouraging new entrants to outdoor education, although, even in the late 1970s, trainees were not automatically expected to acquire the NGB awards.

One beneficiary of the trainee scheme under Bill March was Simon Powell. Simon met Bill when he attended a Rock Instructors' course when he was just 17. Subsequently, he took his ML Introductory and started at Plas y Brenin as a barman a fortnight later, combining it with on-the-job instructor training. Over the course of the next twelve months, his role gradually evolved into a fully instructional one, albeit without having had the opportunity to gain any NGB awards. He worked mostly on the mountaineering and climbing side but gained experience in canoeing as well. In 1978, Simon moved from Plas y Brenin to work for Outward Bound. By the time he opened Mountaincraft in 1986, he had built up his NGB awards, including attending the first Winter MIC course at Glenmore Lodge. In 1989, Simon Powell drafted the idea for the creation of an Association for MIC holders. He quickly gained support from Doug Jones (then Deputy Principal of Marle Hall and currently County Officer for Outdoor Education for Bedfordshire and a Director of the Mountain Training Trust) and, as a result, the Association of Mountain Instructors (AMI) was launched. It now has over 1000 members - MIC and MIA holders - and represents their interests.

The mid-1970s remained a time of rapid change although much of it was cosmetic without affecting the running of the Centre or the success of its courses. Within a very short time, job titles and roles changed once more. Bill March found himself titled Director again but the biggest alteration was the division of the Chief Instructor and Deputy Director's role into two separate posts. Roger Orgill became Deputy Director and Dave Alcock was promoted to Chief Instructor and the Senior Instructor's post fell by the wayside. The VIs and emporary instructors were re-titled Trainee Instructors. Most VIs still worked for 2-4 week periods and their evel of responsibility depended on their personal reputations.

At this point the Centre also underwent another name change, becoming Plas y Brenin National Centre for Mountain Activities. In reality, the name changes probably made little impact. To the climbing world, it was still simply "the Brenin" but, in this instance, there was sound reasoning behind it. The Recreational Charities Act did not look favourably on single activity centres that fell within its purview and the alteration was to fend off any unwarranted criticism of the Centre's status. Plas y Brenin had never been purely a mountaineering centre and the new name was felt to reflect the diversity of its work more accurately.

Bill March resigned from his post as Director in 1977 and Roger Orgill became Acting Director, with Dave Alcock his Acting Deputy. When he worked at Glenmore Lodge, Bill had met Harrison "H" Hilbert, at that time the Director of the Idaho State University Outdoor Program, and that meeting resulted in him doing research under the auspices of a graduate assistantship. Bill had gained his Masters from Idaho State University and, after leaving Plas y Brenin, returned to North America to work at the University of Calgary. In 1982, he led the first Canadian expedition to Everest although he did not summit himself. In 1990, while leading a group of students, Bill suffered an aneurysm and died. In 1998, some of his ashes were taken to the top of Everest by his friend Tom Whittaker, the first disabled climber to reach the summit. Some were also scattered at Glenmore Lodge and at Plas y Brenin. The Banff Centre has given the Summit of Excellence Award annually since 1987 to individuals who have made a contribution to mountain life in the Canadian Rockies. The recipients are diverse - "Alpinist", "Mother - Mentor - Mountaineer", "Historian - Author - Interpreter" and "Park Warden - Rescue Specialist" are among the designations. The Award was renamed the Bill March Summit of Excellence Award in memory of Bill and in recognition of his love and enthusiasm for the mountains.

Roger Orgill's temporary tenure had to guide Plas y Brenin through a turbulent time when the Centre was affected by clashes between the BMC and the MLTB over the direction it should be taking. The Management Committee's view tended towards that of the MLTB - that training was the way forward - while the BMC favoured Plas y Brenin being a centre of excellence for rock climbing. At the root of the problem was the financial situation as it was public money that was funding Plas y Brenin through the Sports Council. For both organisations, the appointment of a new Director to replace Bill March was crucial with each wanting "their" man in post.

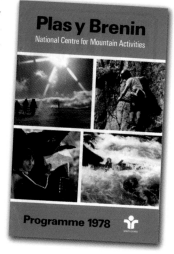

Despite these difficulties, Plas y Brenin did not stagnate under its temporary leadership. There was a slight shift away from the most specialised rock climbing courses and towards those at a more basic level. Orienteering was expanding, and continued to do so for many years. The British Orienteering Federation helped with the preparation of new maps, sending a student to work at Plas y Brenin for a month, and by 1979 it was obvious that a full time orienteer was required on the staff.

Mountain Art and Photography, and Mountain Weather were added to the programme. Both were courses aimed at increasing people's enjoyment of the mountains, broadening the Centre's horizons to accommodate those who wished to experience the environment without necessarily combining that with the hard skill needed for some activities. Mountain Weather had the added advantage of being extremely useful to candidates for NGB Awards. Even at ML level, weather forecasting is a requirement.

John Barry arrived at Plas y Brenin in 1978 very much a "new broom" and with the support of the BMC. Like the Centre's first Warden, Gim Milton, Barry came from a military background and, at the time of his appointment, he was a serving Marine with a good reputation as a climber. His start date at Plas y Brenin had to be put back to accommodate his discharge from the armed forces.

From the very beginning, Barry was trying to fulfil a difficult remit because of the different organisations that had an interest in Plas y Brenin and their diverse agendas. While the Sports Council obviously wanted to ensure maximum income to justify their involvement with the Centre, the BMC were looking more towards specialist courses and Barry had to do his best to comply with the demands made on him. His methods were, at times, unorthodox, but he succeeded in hitting the targets he was presented with in terms of revenue even when the interested parties were finding it difficult to work in harmony.

The Management Committee had set up a Working Party to "consider representations from interested bodies, organisations and individuals concerning the purpose, work and future development of Plas y Brenin as the National Centre for Mountain Activities". In due course, a substantial increase in leadership courses was recommended. This was in line with the Centre's original aims.

John Barry at the Kendal Mountain Film Festival in the 1980's

Changes at the Sports Council resulted in an alteration in the way Plas y Brenin handled capital investment projects. Rather than having a rolling budget, with scheduled work simply continuing until it was completed, budgets were to be set for a twelve month period with unspent monies returned. To ensure that the Centre could take the best advantage of available funding, even if a planned job had to be delayed or overran the end of the financial year, capital projects were divided into priority categories. This meant that, if a hold-up occurred with ongoing work, it was possible for a decision to be made about transferring the budget to another project without needing to await the next Management Committee meeting.

In addition to the Sports Council funding and the Centre's own income, the Whitbread Sports Fund still continued to give grants to assist with Plas y Brenin's work. In 1980 they provided £1,000 towards a course for leaders working in

deprived areas of the West Midlands. This was followed up within a matter of months by a second grant to enable children from these areas to actually attend a course at the Centre. While the leadership course was a success, the course for the youngsters was difficult and motivating the students proved very demanding indeed. This led to some debate about concerns that the main beneficiaries of Plas y Brenin's work were middle class and the Sport For All ethos was failing to reach the disadvantaged. However, with almost half the courses run at the Centre being teaching and leadership based it was obvious that there was an ongoing knock-on effect to many others. This would undoubtedly include those who did not

Sir Jack Longland, Chairman of the Management Committee 1965 - 1980

particularly reap rewards from attending a course at the Centre themselves.

In 1980, after many years of service on the Management Committee, Sir Jack Longland retired as Chairman and was replaced by an old friend of Plas y Brenin - former Deputy Warden John Disley.

While John Barry's years as Director of Plas y Brenin are possibly remembered as being amongst the most difficult in the Centre's history, his active encouragement with regard to staff development saw many instructors grabbing opportunities to extend their own experiences on expedition, including Barry himself. And it was not just the permanent staff who benefited. The Trainees found themselves revamped for the second time in a very short interval, becoming Aspirant Instructors. In return for six months' work on minimal pay, they now received the opportunity to acquire their NGB awards. It was close to what March had envisaged but had not fully implemented during his tenure. John Barry admits he "probably stole" this idea from his predecessor!

The away courses continued to develop under John, who partially closed the Centre for two months in the winter so that the Scottish Winter courses could be expanded. Unfortunately, one result of this was that the improvement in contact with Glenmore Lodge that March had been aiming for was temporarily soured by what was seen as an intrusion into the Lodge's territory. Some of the winter courses were based at Loch Eil, maintaining the long association between Plas y Brenin and the Outward Bound Trust. Meanwhile, a skeleton staff ran the Centre, taking bookings, opening the bar part-time and running some ski courses. Such was the success of this arrangement that the staff were praised for the "goodwill and prestige" brought to the Centre through skiing. Between December and February, those staff who were not required elsewhere visited the Sports Council Regions and inner cities,

John Disley instructing on a Plas y Brenin rock climbing course in the 1950s

promoting Plas y Brenin and outdoor education.

By 1981, the Sports Council for Wales was setting up its own Centre - Plas y Deri - barely 20 miles away on the Menai Straits near Caernarfon. Many Centres had opened since 1955 but a large proportion of them were LEA run or commercial centres that did not impinge on the work of Plas y Brenin. But there were genuine concerns that the two National Centres would find themselves in conflict and the Sports Council agreed to meet with the Sports Council for Wales in order to resolve any problems of duplication before the new Centre opened. Consequently a Joint Co-ordinating Committee was established with one priority being to refute any suggestion that one Centre was for England and one for Wales.

In 1983 Plas y Deri underwent its own name change, becoming Plas Menai. Former Plas y Brenin Director John Jackson was the Centre's first Principal and he was succeeded by Bob Bond in 1985. By then, the two Sports Council Centres were working in harmony, with Plas Menai focusing on watersports.

The number of student beds at the Centre had been increased to 60 and, in an effort to keep running costs within the set parameters, course charges had had to rise. By 1984, the basic daily rate was up to £11.30, plus VAT, and there was little margin for any further increases. Revenue was also being generated by day and evening courses and by the new bunkhouse. The occupancy rate remained encouragingly high and Plas y Brenin was attracting staff of a very high calibre. A survey of students had shown a very high proportion of the respondents were satisfied with what they found at the Centre. Promoting Plas y Brenin became a major

Local children enjoying Plas y Brenin's ski slope

cus and publicity materials were developed in an ffort to increase the number of students. The lecture rogramme continued as a way of spreading the word.

he children's evening classes continued to run, with rienteering courses in addition to skiing. The quality of taffing remained extremely high - Mike Keating and ater Reg Popham worked alongside British Ski Coach ayne Wainwright, co-owner of the Ty'n y Coed Hotel n Capel Curig. The charges were minimal, but the nstruction was at or above the level offered at other venues, and the courses continued to produce a number of excellent skiers, including members of the British Ski Team in the 1980s and 1990s.

Plas y Brenin

National Centre for Mountain Activities 1984

Plas y Brenin suffered the loss of four young instructors in the autumn of 1986 when Ian Fox, Ian Kerr, Dave Woolridge and Steve Briggs went missing while on expedition to Hagshu Peak in the Kishtwar Region of India. There was no evidence of what had happened to the group and others visited the area to try to resolve the mystery, including Ian Fox's parents and Mike Woolridge, Dave's brother and also a Plas y Brenin instructor. There have been separate searches by Paul Nunn and by Issie Inglis, Dave "Smiler" Cuthbertson and John Barry. In 1994 Paul Nunn discovered that someone had found traces of an expedition in the Hagshu Nulla. Later that year he returned with Chris Fox, Ian's brother, and Mandy Glanville, meeting up with John Barry who was already on expedition to Hagshu Peak. Hampered by early snow, they nonetheless managed to recover enough evidence of the quartet's base camp to know where they had been. The remains of a diary finished with an entry for 1 October 1986. There was no trace of the missing climbers or their rucksacks, ropes, boots or climbing equipment but it was possible to pinpoint more closely when and where an event had overwhelmed them. For their families and friends, including many connected with Plas y Brenin, it meant a degree of closure at last.

The senior Plas y Brenin staff underwent some changes during Barry's time as Director. Dave Alcock, who knew he would not be able to extend his contract, decided to leave before it ended, only to be seriously injured when he was avalanched during a Scottish Winter Course in February 1982. Although he returned, Alcock left Plas y Brenin in March of the same year and Dave Walsh replaced him as Chief Instructor.

Roger Orgill, who had been at Plas y Brenin since the day it opened, left the following year to become Director of Outdoor Adventure Activities in the Sports Council's Sport for All campaign. Initially attached to the West Midlands office, when the programme was expanded to the North West, Roger found himself working with several former Brenin students. Later he transferred to the Sports Council Headquarters as Senior Development Officer for Countryside and Water Recreation. This new role enabled him to maintain his links with many former colleagues as his duties included acting as Liaison Officer for many National Governing Bodies. For his long and outstanding service to Outdoor Education, Roger Orgill was awarded the MBE in 1989.

Plas y Brenin's recognition internationally was indicated by its choice as the location of the UIAGM General Council AGM, which was held there in 1984. Four years later, the UIAA Alpinism Committee chose the Centre as the location for its meeting.

At times during his Directorship, John Barry's informal attitude to expedition leave procedures had cause him problems. As it was important to John that his staff maintained their skills, so it was essential that he di the same but it was felt that there had been times when he had been absent from Plas y Brenin without firs making a formal request for leave through the Management Committee. In 1985 he was invited to New Zealand for a lecture tour and applied for leave only to have it refused. He subsequently resigned from post Dave Walsh became Acting Director with Malcolm Campbell stepping up as Acting Chief Instructor to cove the three month gap until the new Director started.

John Barry still lives in North Wales and is a very active mountaineer. He is heavily involved with a freelance risk assessment business, advising corporate clients about potential risks and solutions. He is also well-known as a writer, both individually and as co-author of the classic 'Cold Climbs'.

Only five years after leaving Plas y Brenin, Dave Alcock returned as its fifth Director although his appointment was on a five year contract rather than an open ended one. Dave Alcock, like Bill March before him, was part of a new generation of outdoor educationalists who had emerged after the inception of Plas y Brenin and partly as a result of it. After some time lecturing in engineering, Alcock only moved into a full time career as an instructor in 1973 initially at the Towers, Wolverhampton LEA's centre near Capel Curig. He was working at Plas y Brenin three years later.

The Management Committee also had new leadership. John Disley retired as Chairman and was succeeded by Alan Blackshaw, who was to remain in the position until the whole management hierarchy was restructured in 1996. While Alan was in the chair, the Management Committee became the Plas y Brenin Advisory Committee.

There was a very real need to ensure that new staff matched the quality of the existing instructors and the two day interview was introduced in 1987, whereby a candidate had to provide evidence of their practical skills as well as undergoing a traditional interview. The system was initially used to appoint a female head of orienteering. On the first day, Dave Walsh and Malcolm Campbell took the candidates to the Llanberis slate quarries for a walk where they explored parts that are now closed during an informal "getting to know you"

John Disley retired as chairman in 1987

session. The second day was devoted to the more formal, individual interviews. Anne Salisbury, who had been the 1985 British Elite Orienteering Champion and was a National Orienteering Coach, was the first instructor appointed through the new interview method. A classic example of how Plas y Brenin helped its staff to develop as well as its students, Anne spent five and a half years at the Centre during which she gained her MIC, became the first training officer for the European Mountain Leader Award (EML) and trained and qualified as a user of the Myers Briggs Type Indicator for the facilitation of management training courses. She went on to work at Moray House, part of the University of Edinburgh, including involvement in the establishment of their first ndergraduate degree course in Outdoor Education and Environmental Science before moving on to the dventure Activities Licensing Authority (AALA). Anne was also involved with the children's evening essions in orienteering in the late 1980s, using courses at Plas y Brenin and Nant Bwlch y Hearn, then lwyd's LEA Centre.

urther staff training ventures were also introduced as part of a juggling of senior staff responsibilities. Jnder Dave Alcock's guidance, the Aspirant Instructor scheme was enhanced and continued to generate a egular supply of instructors who had received a solid grounding for their careers, with NGB awards ombined with a period of work experience that was unmatched elsewhere. Other staff training was estructured into a progressive programme that did not simply include the instructional staff enhancing their qualifications or experience. Customer care, financial management and marketing and presentation and psychology were to be included although everyone felt it was important for Plas y Brenin to maintain its traditional frontier spirit. Looking back from 2005, it is possible to see how this strategy successfully helped to guide Plas y Brenin to its current market standing.

The domestic staff also underwent a major transition during Dave's tenure as their roles were determined to fall into the area that the Sports Council had decided required competitive tendering. While this move was designed to make all Sports Council facilities more cost effective and efficient, in the case of Plas y Brenin, it was difficult to administer. The Centre tended to draw on the local community for its domestic staff and it was essential that

Dave Alcock

any company winning the contract to supply Plas y Brenin's catering, cleaning and maintenance staff did not alienate the existing incumbents of those jobs. Any existing employee had to be offered a post by the company winning the tender for services. And, if any chose not to remain under new terms and conditions, there was a limited work force to draw on to replace them. For Alcock, as Centre Director, it also added an extra layer of management in that area whereas both the instructional and some administration staff remained as Sports Council employees. The tender for Catering Cleaning and Maintenance was won by Compass Leisure. Their staff took over a lot of the day to day Centre maintenance - including some work previously undertaken by instructors - and major work was contracted out by the Sports Council. However, perhaps the single biggest effect of contracting out this side of Plas y Brenin was to drastically reduce flexibility - both in terms of how things at the Centre happened but also in the pricing of courses and activities (the contractor having been guaranteed a fixed payment for every overnight stay course/student day).

Plas y Brenin was undergoing more building work as the student accommodation was upgraded to provide en suite rooms for everyone. This led to another clash between the Sports Council and the BMC over the type of facilities that should be available to those attending courses. The cottages previously used for staff accommodation were also developed to provide self-catering facilities that could be booked independently of Plas y Brenin courses. There was also a need to improve disabled access and, while independent grant money was not available for this development the Management Committee did successfully lobby for funding to be provided from the Sports Council's special subventions, rather than needing to find it in Plas y Brenin's revenue budget. By 1989, a new bar and lecture room were complete and were officially opened by Sir Chris Bonington, whose skill at not only leading expeditions but also promoting them had made a major

Chris Bonington

contribution to the public's changed perceptions of mountaineering. Eloquent and knowledgeable Chris was - and remains - instantly recognisable far beyond the normal parameters of the outdoor world.

Under Dave Alcock's Directorship, the programme was expanded once more, particularly the away courses which now encompassed Spanish Rock Climbing and Alpine Canoeing as well as expeditions to places further afield e.g. Mount Kenya. In 1986, the BMC helped to arrange six joint courses for the following year and, with tensions easing, also participated in a joint working party with Plas y Brenin to consider the Centre achieving parity with Glenmore Lodge for winter training and assessment courses. The six day course format was reduced to five days (with the exception of MLTB courses) so that weekend courses could be expanded in an effort to meet new reduced target deficits in future years. This also enabled Plas y Brenin to introduce courses that had not previously been possible while maintaining the secondary day and evening courses.

In 1987, Plas y Brenin hosted its first Triathlon. The idea was Charlie Trotman's and the event included canoeing on Llynau Mymbr, a road cycle and an ascent of Moel Siabod. Reebok and Karrimor provided sponsorship and prizes. The Sports Council usually arranged for a high ranking athlete to both start the event and present the prizes and the support received from local farmers and the Ogwen Valley Mountain Rescue Organisation helped to make the triathlon a tremendous success. Over the years the competition evolved - road cycling becoming mountain biking - and saw changes in sponsorship, with Nike taking over.

A children's triathlon also attracted interest - their shortened course included swimming across Llynau Mymbr, a loop across the road and running along the track from Jim's Bridge to Plas y Brenin.

At times, Plas y Brenin seemed to suffer from unfair comparison with the other Sports Council National Centres (Crystal Palace, Bisham Abbey, etc). It was unique in needing so many specialised staff but this inevitably put a

Triathlon T-Shirt Poster ~ 1989

train on budgets and even with its subsidies, the Director had to rein in costs to stay within the set parameters. In another effort to achieve the best results for the money invested, it was decided to give more commercial and financial responsibility to the Director.

Shortly afterwards, the Advisory Committee was reorganised so that it continued to provide technical advice and support to the Director but its remit on finance was reduced. While Committee members needed to

The ski slope provides a popular addition to the multi activity and taster programmes which have run successfully since 1989.

be kept apprised of the salient points, the day to day details were to be dealt with by Dave Alcock and the Sports Council directly. The restructured Committee was made up of one Sports Council Board member, one representative from each NGB (MLTB, BCU, BOF and the English Ski Council), two from the BMC, one from the CCPR, one from the Sports Council for Wales and one from the National Centres Board plus the Director of Plas y Brenin, a staff representative and two independent members. Others would be seconded from Plas y Brenin or the Sports Council when necessary. When the reorganisation was duly completed, the new Committee more accurately represented those with a valid interest in Plas y Brenin and also provided the expertise needed if it was to fulfil its advisory role fully. By 1989, the Committee had reduced the frequency of its meetings from three per annum to two, although Dave Alcock sent monthly reports and programmes of forthcoming events to each Committee member.

It was recognised that the specialised excellence provided by Plas y Brenin had a relatively small market and so some aspects of its work had to be seen as loss-leaders and set against the other courses, especially those focused on training. Plas y Brenin was deemed to present an appropriate role model - remaining a Centre of Excellence in its field even after more than 30 years. The Sports Council knew it could rely on that established reputation when the Centre's aims were redefined - that it should provide "a multi-faceted environment within which individuals may safely attain the standard of personal performance in mountain and mountain related activities to which they aspire". While marketing it effectively was essential to maintain maximum revenue, providing a higher excellence content was even more important than an excellence image.

By the late 1980s "risk assessment" and "safety" were the new buzzwords in outdoor education. With ever more participants eager to pursue adventurous activities, there was plenty of scope for growth in the market, which inevitably led to some less scrupulous operators. At

Plas y Brenin, working without the appropriate safety boundaries was simply not considered. In 1987 small Standing Safety Committee was set up to consider all the elements of the activities offered in an effort to ensure that unnecessary risk was eliminated. Initially, the Safety Committee's role was to examine the individual activities and create guidelines but they also reviewed accidents and accident procedures at the Centre. Their first report indicated that 77% of all accidents at Plas y Brenin occurred on the ski slope, but many were very minor (the figure reduced to 40% by the following year); the second highest accident figure was in orienteering. For a centre renowned for activities that are often perceived by the public to be dangerous, it showed they had an outstanding record in those areas that were most high risk.

As early as 1990, suggestions were put forward for an accreditation scheme for commercial providers of outdoor pursuits in an effort to weed out the unscrupulous. While the matter came under discussion, at the time the number of incidents involving commercial centres was quite small. However, after the Lyme Bay tragedy in 1993, in which four teenage students from a commercial centre died in a canoeing accident, formal legislation was brought in with the passing of the Activity Centres (Young Persons Safety) Act 1995 and licensing began. Following the formation of AALA, all commercial centres offering adventure activities to young people outside certain tight parameters were required to apply for a licence, which has to be renewed on a regular basis.

The close association between Plas y Brenin and the BMC and NGBs meant that the Centre was able to offer assistance when it became necessary to expand the existing office space at the BMC in Manchester. Rather than simply finding new premises in the same location to solve the overcrowding problem, a section of the old ski store at Plas y Brenin was converted to create a new base for the MLTB. North Wales has the highest concentration of ML providers in the UK and moving the base to the National Mountain Centre was an ideal and logical step. The offices quickly expanded and one of the old staff cottages - Siabod - is now home to MLTE, MLTW, BMG, AMI and BAIML. For both providers and candidates, it is a much more suitable location than Manchester city centre and all are welcome to drop in.

There had been an increase in the number of climbing walls in the UK and the BMC were aware that a time may come when competitive climbing would emerge. At this embryonic stage in the sport, they issued a recommendation that events should only take place on artificial structures. Development of the idea was very rapid indeed, with the emergence of national and international competitions and Plas y Brenin decided that they should include competition climbing judging and coaching in their staff training in future. Over the following 15 years, competitive climbing expanded with Britain producing some outstanding champions. Whether they compete or not, many who use climbing walls do not make the transition to crags, and Plas y renin helps to bridge that gap for those who would like to venture outside, running courses covering every aspect of rock climbing for those with some experience on artificial walls.

No Centre is immune to the possibility of tragedy striking although, thankfully, it is very rare. On 28 September 1992, Plas y Brenin suffered the terrible loss of four members of staff in an air crash near Kathmandu. Mick and Sue Hardwick, Dave Harries and Alison Cope all worked on the instructional staff; Mick was head of the Rock department and Dave was in charge of Scottish Winter and Alpine Climbing and Skiing. Quite apart from the significant loss in staffing, their deaths hit those remaining very hard indeed. All good centres build a sense of family within their staff and friendships are forged that last a lifetime. Many instructors both work and play together, spending leisure and social time with one another whether it is simply an evening's climbing locally or a major expedition to the greater ranges. To lose four colleagues so abruptly inevitably put Plas y

Martin Doyle on the summit of Everest 1999

Brenin into a long recovery period. The families of those who died set up the Kathmandu Memorial Bursary, which provides awards biannually to help fund students on NGB courses.

Nick Banks had returned to Plas y Brenin in 1987 and became Chief Instructor following Dave Walsh's departure in 1990. In 1994, Nick left, another casualty of an unsuccessful leave application when he wanted to lead a commercial expedition to Everest's North Ridge, and Martin Doyle became Chief Instructor. Within a very short time he was appointed Director when Dave Alcock retired just a year later.

Dave took early retirement with the intention of combining some large projects on his home with trips to the mountains. He has not been lured back to work the way John Jackson was, but has simply carried on making the most of his retirement. His climbing trips include the Lotus Flower Tower in the Canadian NW Territories, Wind Rivers in Wyoming and Mount Whitney and Yosemite in California.

Like Jacko, Martin Doyle had been a geography teacher prior to moving into outdoor education. Having worked as Senior Instructor at Whernside Manor, Martin joined the staff at Glenmore Lodge in 1987. Two years later, now a fully qualified Guide, Martin formed a guiding and adventure company. It was a move that provided a steep learning curve in all aspects of training, marketing, budgeting and management. The opportunity to work at the other National Centre and concentrate on the training aspects presented itself and Martin started at Plas y Brenin in March 1992.

By 1993, Martin was in charge of Alpine mountaineering and ski mountaineering as well as running the newly introduced MIA scheme. He was a natural successor to Nick Banks as Chief Instructor. Appointed

Acting Centre Director in the spring of 1994, Martin became Director in June of that year.

No previous Director had inherited the Centre at such a difficult time. From its current position it is perhaps hard to believe that, just a decade ago, there was a real possibility that Plas y Brenin would close. In terms of facilities, staff and courses, the Centre was as successful as ever, but the problems behind the scenes were making everyone increasingly nervous. Business was being limited by the restraints put on budgets and staffing levels and these outside factors were having an adverse effect on the Brenin's reputation simply because it was not able to meet the demand for courses.

Changes in the NGB awards increased the pressure. The Single Pitch Supervisor's Award (SPSA - now the SPA) was introduced in 1992 and the MIC was split into two parts. While the MIC remained in place, a lower level that did not cover winter mountaineering came into being - the Mountain Instructor's Award (MIA).

The Sports Council needed to reduce the proportion of its budget that was spent on administration in order to increase funding to sports development. Plas y Brenin inevitably came under scrutiny, along with other Sports Council projects, and a staffing cap was put in place as the situation was reviewed.

The split contract system - with catering, cleaning and maintenance run by an outside contractor - had been unsettling and lacked flexibility towards the director and management of the centre, but it was obvious that the Sports Council could make savings by also contracting out for the technical and administration staff roles. Through the latter half of 1995 and into 1996, the complicated process of finding someone to take over progressed, with an eventual short list of five parties that had registered interest. One of these - Mountain Centres Management Limited (MCM) had been set up by Alan Blackshaw specifically to run the Brenin. Four companies, including MCM, eventually tendered to run the Management Contract. Only one, from Glendale Leisure Limited, came close to what the Sports Council felt was needed. In April 1996, they were offered the contract but it quickly became apparent that they were unlikely to be able to deliver their management strategy.

Faced with a loss of morale amongst the staff and an uncertain future, the Advisory Committee of Plas y Brenin took the step of lobbying government in order to block the transfer to Glendale Leisure. The national governing bodies had a vested interest in maintaining the status quo at the Centre. Their backing - combined with that of Martin Doyle and the Centre staff - helped, and the negotiations broke down. But the difficulties faced by the Sports Council were still not resolved and the process of finding someone to run the Centre restarted. Once again, several companies were prominent amongst the bidders.

By now, a working party had been set up to look at Plas y Brenin's priorities, concluding that three areas needed particular consideration -

• guiding principles

• work priorities

• associated activities and issues.

It was becoming obvious that those whose hearts lay closest to the Centre would best fulfil the role of caretakers. Consequently, a charitable trust was set up by the BMC, the MLTB and the UKMTB for the specific purpose of running the National Mountain Centre. By September 1996, the newly incorporated ountain Training Trust (MTT) had ibmitted its formal tender for the 1anagement Contract of Plas y renin, it was accepted and they)ok over officially in January 1997.

Iain Peter high on Cerro Torre 2005

1artin Doyle's tenure as Director of 'las y Brenin was relatively short ompared with most of his >redecessors. In the midst of the segotiations for the Management Contract, he succeeded in keeping Plas y Brenin focused and working without falter. Many of the staff had become demoralised and that could have been allowed to affect courses and students negatively. But the day to day running of the Centre continued uninterrupted. Undoubtedly, this stood in Plas y Brenin's favour as time progressed. If the quality of staffing and courses remained undiminished, then it was possible to remain optimistic.

Martin's influence was seen in the significant expansion of the Alpine courses and he also encouraged the British Mountain Guide (BMG) courses to use the Centre. Over the years, many of the staff had held the prestigious Guide's award and strengthening the links with an international organisation of their standing could only enhance the Brenin's reputation. As a member of the BMG Training Committee and Convenor for their Summer Assessment courses, Martin was ideally placed to capitalise on that.

The changeover from the Bangor Mountaineering First Aid course to the REC course took place, a venture that has been built on since so that Plas y Brenin can now provide over 450 places per annum. Martin ensured that the winter mountaineering element of the MIC was also reintroduced, as part of the larger Scottish Winter Programme. By the time Iain Peter arrived as CEO, Martin Doyle had led Plas y Brenin through its most turbulent time and taken it from a very real threat of closure to a point where its future was brighter than ever. When both the staff at the Centre and those responsible for Plas y Brenin's very existence needed it most, he offered a steady, guiding hand on the helm.

The Staff

As with any outdoor centre, Plas y Brenin's strength lies in its staff. Whether it is in the middle of a city or in the perfect rural environment, what a centre offers - and its reputation - is dependent on both the instructional and background staff combining their individual talents with the resources available to them. From the day it opened, Plas y Brenin recognised this, which was why Emrys Roberts was retained from the staff of the old Royal Hotel as Bursar for the new Centre. And the use of permanent instructional staff from the beginning enabled it to offer courses that would have been impossible with a different set up. The creation and awarding of National Governing Body qualifications helped Plas y Brenin to be seen as the centre of excellence that was envisaged from the earliest discussions about its role in the outdoor world.

The need for development was also identified, so that instructional staff were not only the best available at any given time, but there was also the means to train them within the Centre itself. Today, a multitude of people - from a variety of backgrounds and at all levels of outdoor education - owe something to Plas y Brenin as they have been Volunteer, Trainee or Aspirant Instructors there; or they have attended a course - anything from the most basic introduction to an activity to the assessment for their MIC, a Guide's course or a BCU Coaching Award; or they have worked there as an instructor and been allowed the opportunity to develop themselves during that employment.

When Gim Milton was appointed as the first Warden, he had an instructional staff of just three - John Disley, Tim Aron and Roger Orgill. Sheila Deans was later appointed as the first female instructor. In 2005, Plas y Brenin's instructors have increased tenfold and, between them, can muster 27 MICs, 11 Guides' carnets and nine BCU Level 5 Coaching Awards.

In addition to the permanent staff, the Centre relied on Voluntary Instructors - those willing to donate their time to help teach others. A VI could work for as short a period as a week or as long as a year, receiving in return very little in terms of wages - £1 to £4 at first - together with their board and lodging. For many it was a golden opportunity to spend some time in the heart of the mountains rather than snatching a weekend's climbing whenever they could. And the experience gained could, and often did, lead to a new career. When ley had free time, the VIs would inevitably be out enjoying their surroundings, whether they were climbing, canoeing or simply seeing how far they could stretch their wages in one of Capel Curig's bars. Today, a VI working in a centre would expect more than was received in the 1950s, but even as recently as that there was feeling that the value of the bed and board provided was equal to a salary. Those who could avail themselves of the situation tended to come from more monied backgrounds although anyone in domestic service would be in a similar situation. The domestic staff also had what was effectively a VI system in place under Gim Milton. In their case, it was in the form of an au pair scheme that brought them from several European countries. Some returned home afterwards, some settled in Wales or elsewhere in the UK.

Staff conditions were very different - some of the benefits that are considered to be standard now were virtually unheard of less than 50 years ago. It was not until 1958 that the Management Committee granted the staff a holiday entitlement and two thirds of it was set to fit around the Centre's programme.

The same year saw the first major staff changes as both Tim Aron and Sheila Deans left that year and were replaced by Brian Grey and Jo Scarr. Also in 1958, Alex Baines was appointed as Storeman, the title given at that time to any centre's ubiquitous jack-of-all-trades. The Storeman is invariably responsible for the maintenance and distribution of equipment, and for dealing with offenders (whether staff or students) who fail to care for their temporary possessions in a suitable manner. Alex remained at Plas y Brenin until 1972 and, during his time there, the "stores" expanded to include all of the Centre's vehicles as well.

The situation remained little changed until 1969 when it was agreed that Plas y Brenin required a sixth permanent staff member. By then, John "Jacko" Jackson was Director and the Centre had built a strong reputation and its business was growing rapidly. Plas y Brenin continued to go through a series of transitions, including many changes in personnel, but the tenor of its permanent staff were the foundations of its success and remain so even today.

The reputation of the individuals has always been a major factor in the growing development of Plas y Brenin. Many have brought with them impressive CVs and are able to apply skills garnered across the globe in their teaching. Many built on the instructional reputations gained while employed at Plas y Brenin - names familiar both to those working in the field of outdoor education and to the public in general. And not everyone specialised in only outdoor activities.

The Plas y Brenin staff line-up in 2005

A freestyle kayaking course with Loel Collins at Plas y Brenin

John Disley was probably better known as an athlete than an instructor. In 1955, while working at Plas y Brenin, he broke the World Record for the 3000m steeplechase and was Athlete of the Year. For many, his name is most closely associated with orienteering. John introduced the activity in England and has links with the very foundations of its structure, seeing it develop from a "new" sport to the widespread participation that it has today. And for others, his name is always linked with the London Marathon. In 1981, John was a Founder Director, with Chris Brasher, of the event - the world's largest marathon - and he remains Chairman of the London Marathon Trust, which distributes surplus funds raised by the race to sport and recreation provision in the city. By 2005 over £16m had been donated and the future should see sufficient funds available to maintain the 2012 Olympic Indoor Sports Complex as a Legacy site.

Success in their individual fields has also enabled others to gain a reputation away from specific instructional roles. Many Plas y Brenin staff have written about their experiences or used the medium to pass on their expertise. Steve Long, who joined Plas y Brenin staff in 1993, is not only a Guide with a varied career and Arctic and Antarctic experience, but is also the author of 'Hillwalking', one of a series of definitive manuals produced by MLTUK. 'Rock Climbing' written by Libby Peter and published by MLTUK in 2005, has quickly become a best seller. Malcolm Creasey, also a Guide, has a wealth of freelance and centre based experience, including several spells at Plas y Brenin, and is currently MLTE Development Officer. As author of 'The Complete Rock Climber', Malc has passed along his experience to many. John Barry's autobiographical 'The Great Climbing Adventure' chronicles his extensive experience climbing throughout the world. He is also co-author of the classic

Steve Long's Hillwalking and Libby Peter's Rock Climbi

Cold Climbs' with his fellow Plas y Brenin Director Dave Alcock nd Ken Wilson, who was a member of the Management Committee for many years. Plas y Brenin CEO Iain Peter's Handbook of Climbing' covers all aspects of climbing and has become the definitive text in its field. Rob Collister, now a freelance Guide, who worked at Plas y Brenin from 1978 to 1987, described his own experiences in 'Over the Hills and Far Away'. Franco Ferraro, head of canoeing from 1993 - 2003 has gone on to develop a highly successful niche publishing business specialising in paddling coaching, safety and instruction manuals. Many other insructors have either writing credits themselves or have contributed to instructional and guide books.

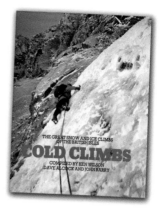

Cold Climbs ~ a well established classic

Plas y Brenin is frequently called on to assist with other media work, often providing safety cover for television and video productions, including personnel doubling for actors when necessary. When they are offered, some staff have taken advantage of other opportunities to appear in front of the camera, as extras in major productions filmed in North Wales, including 'Willow'. Ann Redman was a member of the first women's expedition to the Karakorum, which received wide media coverage including newspaper and magazine articles away from the normal outdoor press. The team's film, documenting their achievements, went on to win the Mick Burke Award.

Canoeist Derek Mayes successfully completed the first canoe crossing - in under 21 hours - of the Irish Sea from Dublin to Holyhead in 1969. His companions on the trip were fellow Plas y Brenin instructor David Bland and Nick Gough, who worked at the Centre from 1974 until 1980. The Management Committee sent their congratulations to the trio, complimenting them particularly on their "strict adherence to safety precautions, which it was hoped would be an example to other canoeists". In 1980, Nigel Timmins was part of the expedition that completed the first successful descent of the Dudh Kosi. Loel Collins has achieved a string of first descents, including the Karon River in Iran, several in the Papua New Guinea Highlands and the two deepest gorges in the world - Cotwahast and Colca Canyons in Peru. Jim Hargreaves was the first person to paddle around Cape Horn and the first Briton to descend the Colorado river. Ray Rowe is not only an accomplished canoeist and instructor but a writer and an Irish Olympic Canoe Team Coach. Pete Catteral successfully made the first descent of the Siang and Lohit Rivers in Arunache Pradesh and also applies his coaching skills away from the

Pete Catterall- Great Britain Freestyle Kayak Team Coach

Iain and Sally Peter relaxing on the slopes of Moel Siabod

Centre, taking charge of the British Kaya Freestyle Team. Leo Hoare also worked as National Coach, of both the Welsh and British Slalom Teams.

When Plas y Brenin opened, the excitement of the first ascent of Everest had not fully abated. Fifty years later the mountain has been climbed by a variety of routes but has never become merely one more ascent to be ticked off. Many staff have reached the summit, including Martin Doyle - whose other achievements in the highest ranges include Vinson in Antarctica, Denali in Alaska and Kilimanjaro - Martin Barnicott, Nick Banks, John Barry, Dave Walsh and Peter Boardman. The latter is amongst the best known British mountaineers. Pete was a member of the 1975 South-West face of Everest expedition and was BMC National Officer and President of the BMG. He moved to Switzerland to take over the Directorship of the International School of Mountaineering in Leysin following the death of Dougal Haston in 1977 and lost his own life five years later on the North-East ridge of Everest when he went missing with Joe Tasker (also a Plas y Brenin temporary instructor). Both were accomplished authors - Boardman wrote The Shining Mountain and Sacred Summits - and their names live on in the prestigious Boardman-Tasker Award for Mountain Literature.

In the early 1960s, Jo Scarr and Barbara Spark embarked on a low budget expedition to the Kulu Himalaya. They drove out alone and, with only Sherpa support, completed several first ascents before joining Countess Dorothia Gravina's all women expedition in Nepal. When they returned, Jo wrote 'Four Miles High', an account of their exploits. She subsequently moved to Australia to work at Canberra University where, in a shift in career, she became an authority on Australian Aboriginal culture.

Rob Spencer climbed Masherbrum II via a new route in 1991 and, a year later, achieved the summit of Rakiot by another new route. Dave Walsh had previously been the first Briton to reach the top of Nanga Parbat and he also made the first solo ascent of Cho Oyo in 1988. In 1995 Norman Croucher - who, while never a member of the instructional staff, was so instrumental in the establishment of courses for the disabled at Plas y Brenin - also reached the summit of Cho Oyo, climbing without oxygen. Iain Peter, who also summited, led the expedition.

Plas y Brenin staff have not only been active on big mountains there have been many notable ascents of Alpine Routes and Big Walls with Mike Turner and Louise Thomas being particularly active. Their ascents in Greenland, on Baffin and in Africa are very significant. In 2005 Steve Long, Neil Johnson and Iain Peter made the first all British ascent of Cerro Torre in Patagonia

From John Jackson's earliest forays in the greater ranges, predating his time at Plas y Brenin, the climbers on the staff have achieved a high level of success producing both first ascents and first British ascents on almost every continent. Check the guidebooks for any British climbing area and there will almost certainly be Plas y Brenin instructors included in the lists of those credited with new routes. The major European and North American routes - including the North Face of the Eiger, the Walker Spur on the Grande Jorasses, the Nose of El Capitan and Half Dome in Yosemite - also feature prominently in their résumés.

is often the case that Plas y Brenin's instructors are ⸿tively involved elsewhere in outdoor education. ⸿heir experience is of enormous benefit to their ⸿ofessional organisations and the National ⸿overning Bodies. As well as Pete Boardman, Rob ⸿ollister, Nigel Shepherd and Nick Banks have all ⸿een President of the BMG. Dave Alcock was Vice ⸿hairman of the MLTB and Martin Doyle currently ⸿hairs MLTE. Dave Humphries spent some time as ⸿ILTB Secretary and John Cousins is Secretary of ⸿ILTUK, a full-time position. John Garside is ⸿raining Officer for both MLTE and the BMC and ⸿hil Thomas fulfils the same role for MTLW. In ⸿ecent years, Plas y Brenin has been able to provide ⸿nany of the NGBs with a base, simplifying their ⸿ogistical arrangements.

⸿Marcus Baillie left Plas y Brenin in 1988 to become ⸿he Director of Tiglin, the National Adventure Centre ⸿or Ireland, and then became Head of Inspection ⸿Services for the Adventure Activities Licensing ⸿Authority. His inspectorate includes many associated ⸿with Plas y Brenin, including Malcolm Campbell and ⸿Anne Salisbury.

Louise Thomas 'Big Walling' on Baffin Island

As Outdoor Education has expanded and developed, more and more openings in the higher levels of education have been created. Inevitably, names familiar at Plas y Brenin have become equally familiar in this field. ABill March was a major contributor to OE in Canada during his time as Director of the Department at the University of Calgary; Barbara (née Spark) and Don Roscoe have inspired a generation of fledgling instructors, having established the Post Graduate Certificate in Outdoor Education at the University College of North Wales, with Tim Jepson taking over after Barbara's retirement; Dave Bland became a lecturer at I M Marsh and Mark Baker, Liz Campbell (née Colthurst) and the late Terry Storry are also closely associated with higher education.

In 1955, the British public was entranced by the achievements of the expeditions that were conquering the world's highest peaks, which contributed to the urge to answer the lure of the mountains in greater and greater numbers in the following years. Five decades later, significant achievements by Britain's mountaineers and paddlers still warrant media attention, although the days of the big expeditions have passed, at least temporarily. When success comes, those who attain it are often self-deprecating and reluctant to capitalise to the fullest extent. If it was possible to dissect the CV of each individual, there's a distinct possibility that Plas y Brenin's name would emerge somewhere either as the venue for a course or a place of work for many. To catalogue everyone would be impossible but, certainly where the staff are concerned, the constant striving for one more new route, one more summit or one more descent are what has always ensured that Plas y Brenin reaps real dividends from its instructors' activities outside the Centre.

From Strength to Strength

Iain Peter came to Plas y Brenin with a proven track record as a mountaineer and in the field of training and "outdoor business". After a decade working as a freelance Guide - including nine winter seasons at Glenmore Lodge and time at the International School of Mountaineering in Leysin - Iain became Training Administrator for the BMC. In this role, he was instrumental in the reconstruction of mountaineering training qualifications. In 1993, he became Executive Secretary of the UKMTB and combined that role with freelance consultancy work. He has always climbed and skied extensively throughout the world including the first British ascents of Gasherbrum 2 (with a ski descent) and Pik Pobeda. Amongst many other successful expeditions, Iain has climbed Mount McKinley, the Nose on El Cap and the North Face of the Eiger.

It was the first time in nearly 20 years that the head of centre was appointed from outside the existing Plas y Brenin staff and, while the ethos of the Centre remained unaltered, the whole management structure went through a period of change that heralded a fresh start. When the Sports Council first awarded a five year management contract to the Mountain Training Trust it marked the start of a new era for the Centre - the whole staff (catering, domestic, instructional, maintenance and administration) were once again united into a single team working for a single employer. This brought new focus and sense of purpose to the operation.

Iain's title was Chief Executive Officer rather than Director and he was answerable to the MTT Board. Martin Doyle became Director of Training with overall responsibility for all instructional matters, including those related to Health and Safety. Two new key positions were created - Financial Controller and Facilities Manager - each with very distinct roles to fulfil. While Plas y Brenin remained under the umbrella of Sport England, with the management contract renewable after five years, its day to day running was now MTT's responsibility and totally on site. A lot of decisions that had previously had to be made at a remote level were now in Iain's hands. The Advisory Committee also remained in place, its remit to advise the Sports Council what Plas y Brenin should be doing and to measure how successful it is at achieving results. While there have been some adjustments over the intervening years, mainly to strengthen the management team as the centre has become busier, this structure continues today.

The first task of the new management team was to lift morale amongst the staff. Working together, a dynamic stance from the very beginning ensured that the Centre remained focused and built on the existing team spirit. The feeling of being under siege lifted as Plas y Brenin re-established itself within its community. In many ways, the management returned to the tried and tested methods from Plas y Brenin's earliest days. Staff were recruited locally where possible and, increasingly, local suppliers and services replaced others.

An open door policy ensured that Plas y Brenin did not stand apart. A concerted effort was made to make climbers, hillwalkers and mountaineers consider Plas y Brenin their Centre and get them to use it. The climbing wall is open for public sessions, the bar is open to all and discounted bed and breakfast is available for BMC and BCU members when Plas y Brenin is not fully booked. Clubs and associations are actively encouraged to consider Plas y Brenin as a venue for annual dinners and meetings and the standard offered easily matches that provided by hotels. The Trust reinstated the Community Dinner, with a free bar - not even the Directors would dare to ask the budget! - and this opportunity to thank those who helped the Centre's existence is now a well established fixture on the winter calendar. The winter lecture programme was also reintroduced.

One major development, which has contributed significantly in encouraging greater use of Plas y Brenin, was at Bryn Engan. The site had more or less fallen into disuse and become primarily a storage facility. For what had previously been such a useful addition to the Centre, this was unacceptable. A major refurbishment was undertaken, with funding from MTT, Sport England and the Forestry Commission. Bryn Engan was converted to provide a self-contained unit accommodating up to 16 people. The official opening was conducted by the Minister for Sport, Richard Caborn MP, on 26 September 2002. Visiting groups can work independently of Plas y Brenin or turn to the Centre and its staff and resources for assistance when required. Bryn Engan is particularly well suited for environmental studies, providing excellent opportunities for residential rural and woodland studies. The local community council recognised this value and it is in regular use by Youth Service groups and as an outreach facility for community projects. The facility is also popular with Scout and Guide groups and Duke of Edinburgh Award Scheme parties. Plas y Brenin also use the Bryn Engan for their young persons' courses. Much of the youth provision is overseen by the Centre's Youth Development Officer, Lissie Smith and Helen Barnard, the Duke of Edinburgh's Award Officer.

As Plas y Brenin moved into the 21st century, it was once again driving forward as a leader in its field. The new management hierarchy was established and the inter-linked departments worked effectively. Every aspect of the Centre was covered and an aura of calm professionalism greets each new student.

Foot and Mouth:

"Everything around here, from pubs to the post office and petrol station, relies on the trade we bring in. With nobody here, they are starting to feel the pinch. The Government has put in place some stringent powers without thinking of the implications"

Iain Peter - interviewed by Anthony Browne for The Observer, 11 March 2001

Martin Doyle's role has evolved as business has increased; Louise Thomas was appointed to the "new position of Chief Instructor in 2001 and is responsible for quality control in the field, induction instructional staff and the mentoring of Centre Assistants and the Instructor Scheme. Ray Hinton, as Financ Controller, plays a key role in the Management Team, advising on budgets and expenditure, reporting to th Sports Council on financial matters and supporting Iain in reporting to Companies House, the Chari Commissioners and the MTT Board. As MTT has grown and developed, the financial intricacies of runnir a relatively complex business have become more and more involved. With the Centre running under th control of a charitable trust, it is imperative that every financial "i" is dotted and "t" crossed. Since 199 turnover at Plas y Brenin has increased from about £700k pa to £3.5m. Ray also manages the seven stron Customer Services Team. John Wright, who had previously worked for the administration and caterin contractor, initially took on the role of Facilities Manager dealing with Centre maintenance. Following h retirement, his Deputy - Bryn Roberts - became Facilities Manager, combining his great experience in th hotel trade with his local knowledge - he was born and raised in Bala. Bryn's calm efficiency in any situatio is much appreciated by all at the Centre. Rob Spencer has been Operations Manager since 2003. A long term instructor and a Guide, Rob takes charge of Health and Safety around the Centre (non-instructional), store and equipment - including a staff of four - and the Brenin's fleet of vehicles.

For some years, prior to taking up his post at Plas y Brenin, Iain Peter had provided consultancy services t the Cheetham Bell advertising agency assisting with their outdoor clients. The success of this venture led tc Dave Cheetham providing expertise on the practicalities of promoting the Centre. Initially a freelancer, Dave is now employed full time. His original and highly innovative input to the Brenin's media presence has been invaluable, creating the Centre's website and establishing its email newsletter as well as producing extremely effective annual brochures and leaflets. Since everything is now produced in-house, cost effectiveness and flexibility are now much improved.

In 2001 the revitalisation of Plas y Brenin suffered a blow over which it had no control - another foot and mouth epidemic. For the vast majority of the urban-dwelling British public the impact was seen in nightly news reports of fresh outbreaks and the efforts that were being made to stem and deal with the rising numbers of infected animals. But for those living in areas like Snowdonia, the fragile rural economy was teetering on the brink of collapse. In many areas tourism and all the inter-linking industries attached to it were hit much harder than the farming community but it appeared their situation was being overlooked. Certainly, rescue packages were set up to aid farmers, but hotels, guest houses, outdoor pursuits instructors and outdoor centres fell outwith the parameters set in place. The English Tourist Board estimated that countryside tourism in 2001 was worth in the region of £12 billion with business down by 75% in the first quarter alone while farm losses were less than a third of that.

As a major centre in a prime tourist region, Plas y Brenin inevitably felt the effects of the epidemic quickly. Not only was the Centre closed - with no students there was no work for instructors and, more importantly, no income - all its Scottish Winter courses were also cancelled. At what should have been a busy time, Plas y Brenin ground to a halt. For Iain Peter, it was a challenge he could not afford to flinch from and, fortunately, he also recognised the importance to the local community as well as to those under his leadership.

By April, the matter had been raised in the House of Lords, where Liberal-Democrat peer Lord Greaves of Pendle brought the crisis in outdoor education to the attention of the Chamber. Lord Greaves is an active

...mpaigner in matters relating to the countryside and is a climber, hill-walker, geographer and botanist. In ...s contribution to the Lords' debate on the impact of foot and mouth on 4 April 2001, Plas y Brenin was ...ted as a special example, with Lord Greaves estimating that the Centre made a contribution of some £2 ...illion per annum to the local economy, adding that, at that time, it was almost non-functioning. He also ...cognised the urgent need for risk assessment and the reopening of as many footpaths as possible in low-...sk areas. Obviously, farm animals had to be protected, but rural tourism in general and outdoor pursuits in ...articular were in grave danger of suffocating as the crisis went on. Iain's efforts were highlighted. Already ...e had been in discussion with the Welsh Assembly Government (WAG) - the Assembly Member ...epresenting Capel Curig, Lord Dafydd Elis-Thomas, is also the Presiding Officer at WAG and a great friend ...nd supporter of Plas y Brenin. Iain was also involved in discussions with the Snowdonia National Park ...uthority, the Local Authorities, National Trust, Countryside Council for Wales, the Farmers' Union of Wales ...nd the National Farmers' Union. By providing reasoned risk assessments and expertise, Plas y Brenin ...ucceeded in achieving the early opening of some areas. In some of the slate quarries and the coastal ...imestone cliffs temporary fences were erected where necessary to separate climbing from farming. At ...Tremadoc the BMC reopened Bwlch y Moch after reaching an agreement with the neighbouring farmer that ...an electric fence would be put up along the top of the cliff.

With more temporary fencing to create safe access routes through farm land, Plas y Brenin reopened for business having protected not only its own staff's positions but those of many local businesses who were, at least in part, reliant on it. It had not been a solo effort by any means, and perhaps the Brenin's biggest contribution was to provide both a focus and administrative support for an action group that included the local community, local authorities and national agencies, enabling them to agree a sensible, realistic way forward in the crisis.

One benefit from Plas y Brenin's major role in safeguarding both the farmland and its own activities was that it was recognised in Wales as a major contributor, banishing forever the myth that it was simply a government facility to teach tourists to climb. The change of name from the Sports Council to Sport England nearly a decade earlier had done Plas y Brenin few favours in respect of its location in Wales, but it was now firmly established as having far wider relevance there as well as far reaching influence. As a result Plas y Brenin now has strong formal links with both the Sports Council for Wales and the Welsh Assembly Government and has become involved in several policy issues. The Centre also works very closely with Conwy, Gwynedd and Ynys Môn Councils.

In 2003, recognising the lack of Welsh speaking instructors, Plas y Brenin was a key player in the North West Wales Outdoor Partnership, established to help to provide dedicated Welsh speaking outdoor development staff to improve local access to outdoor activities. Plas y Brenin launched an initiative to train the leaders for the project and its own evening and day courses for local youngsters is striving towards the same result.

The following year another scheme took the Centre's reputation for on-the-job training to an entirely new level. While there had been opportunities to gain experience under the watchful eye of high calibre instructors in the past, the Fast Track Instructor Scheme additionally provided a clutch of NGB Awards. For a student dedicated to expanding their own skills to further a career in outdoor education, the scheme is unmatched as the programme is personalised for each individual. And, while the course runs from Monday to Friday over a four month period, living in at Plas y Brenin full time means that there are plenty of opportunities to do

Stuart McAlese and Mike 'Twid' Turner on the summit of The Citadel, Kichatna Spires

what other trainees have done in the past - take advantage of the chance to join in other courses or simply enjoy the proximity of the mountains.

Under MTT's management, one problem that had previously seen well qualified, experienced instructional staff leave before the end of their contracts has been overcome. In the past it was sometimes not possible to give staff long term leave - either paid or unpaid - to enable them to participate in expeditions or other ventures, which had led to some significant departures. Now, all contracts of more than twelve months include the right to unlimited unpaid leave provided it is arranged in advance. This has enabled people to remain in post while also furthering their skills and achievements away from Plas y Brenin.

Some opportunities arise simply through requests for assistance from Plas y Brenin. Staff frequently offer safety cover and additional services to the media. With others specialising in providing the same services to larger budget productions, Plas y Brenin works more frequently with relatively low budget projects. There is a great variety in the specific requirements which could be as diverse as an advert for the Welsh Tourist Board, climbing instruction for a Blue Peter presenter or doubling for someone in a pop video.

The MTT Management is closely linked to the major organisations in mountaineering - the BMC, MLTUK and Mountain Leader Training England (MLTE, formerly the MLTB) each provide one Director. This has resulted in greater links with and provision for these "shareholder" bodies. Plas y Brenin is a base for the biennial BMC International Climbing Meets and provides a home for the offices of the MLTUK, the MLTE and Mountain Leader Training Wales (MLTW) as well as the administration base for the Associations for members of the Mountain Guides, Mountain Instructors and the International Mountain Leaders. The BMC and MCofS have been provided with staff, technical staff and resources to help to produce structional videos in rock climbing, navigation and water hazards as well as the expertise for Hillwalking' - the first of a series of handbooks by the MLTUK for its training schemes. Over the years, the Centre's paddling staff have produced many of the standard text books on white water safety, rolling and coaching techniques. And many members of Plas y Brenin staff sit on committees and training boards and make contributions to the outdoors in general.

It is all too easy to manipulate statistics to ensure a positive outcome but, in the case of Plas y Brenin, no manipulation is required when measuring its success. MTT have to meet annual minimum requirements in terms of the number of NGB award training and assessment students delivered. In 2005, in every category, that minimum requirement was exceeded, in some cases by 100% or more. A total of 1,565 students attended courses leading to or awarding them a qualification - ML, SPA, EML, MI, Orienteering and Canoe/Kayak competency or Coaching awards; the minimum requirement was 1,122. For the Centre's Additional (Value Added) courses, which encompasses all other awards, supporting qualifications such as First Aid or Navigation and all other activities, there is no minimum requirement level. However, for these, nearly 4,000 students attended the Brenin, bringing the total for 2005 to 5,513.

Since 2005 marked the 50th annivesary of the opening of Plas y Brenin, it was decided to commemorate the occasion with a number of events spread throughout the year. The initial planning had to be done well in advance as special anniversary courses were offered, providing opportunities for everyone who wanted to join in the celebrations to do so. The Community Dinner in January brought together many of those who were instrumental in the present day success of Plas y Brenin.

On 7 June 2005 HRH Prince Philip, the Duke of Edinburgh, returned to Plas y Brenin as chief guest at a conference and dinner. The village school in Capel Curig has closed in recent years so there were no flag waving children this time, but the enthusiasm and vision the Prince encountered in the staff would undoubtedly have been as marked as on that earlier visit. During the day, the Prince unveiled a commemerative plaque in the foyer of the Centre.

HRH Prince Philip visits Plas y Brenin as part of the fiftieth year celebrations.

Loel Collins, head of canoeing at Plas y Brenin outlines the finer points of coaching

In November, a special 50th Anniversary Lunch was a chance to reunite old friends and colleagues spanning the entire five decades of the Centre's history. This was followed by an anniversary party that proved to be a testament to Plas y Brenin's place in the hearts of those associated with it as nearly 400 guests arrived to celebrate the milestone. They came from near and far and brought with them memories and anecdotes to share in a convivial atmosphere. Amongst the many guests were John Disley and Roger Orgill, whose association with the Centre reached back to the day it opened. Three past Directors - John Barry, Dave Alcock and Martin Doyle - were also there, linking together the years. One absentee was Gim Milton, who nonetheless summed up the feelings of many by way of some taped recollections saying, "I am proud that I was in at the beginning and proud too of all the people who came after us, and who have made such a success of this splendid enterprise . . . we never dreamed of how far you have taken it".

Chronology

1857 . . . . .Alpine Club founded

1889 . . . . .Scottish Mountaineering Club founded

1895 . . . . .First Physical Education College for women opened

1898 . . . . .Climbers' Club founded

1908 . . . . .Scout Association founded

1909 . . . . .National mountaineering organisation proposed

1910 . . . . .Girl Guides Association founded

1930 . . . . .Youth Hostel Association founded

1933 . . . . .Carnegie College of Physical Education opened in Leeds

1934 . . . . .Central Council of Physical Recreation formed

1935 . . . . .Loughborough College launch one year PE course

1937 . . . . .National Fitness Council promoting health and fitness issues

1941 . . . . .Outward Bound founded, Aberdovey Centre opened

1943 . . . . .CCPR forms Outdoor Activity Advisory Committee

1944 . . . . .Standing Advisory Committee on Mountaineering created, evolving into The British
Mountaineering Council the same year

1947 . . . . .Mountaineering Association founded

1948 . . . . .Glenmore Lodge opened in Aviemore

. . . . .CCPR runs first women's climbing course in North Wales

1949 . . . . .CCPR extended to include Northern Ireland

1951 . . . . .First LEA Centre - White Hall in Derbyshire - opened

1953 . . . . .First ascent of Everest, expedition led by Sir John Hunt

1955 . . . . .Plas y Brenin opened in Capel Curig

. . . . .G I "Gim" Milton appointed as Warden of Plas y Brenin

1956 . . . . .Duke of Edinburgh's Award Scheme inaugurated

1960 . . . . .John "Jacko" Jackson appointed Director of Plas y Brenin

1964 . . . . .Mountain Training Board formed

. . . . .Mountain Leadership Certificate launched

1965 . . . . .Mountain Instructor Certificate launched

. . . . .Sports Council founded

1968 . . . . .Mountaineering Association becomes part of Youth Hostel Association

1970 . . . . .Mountaineering Council of Scotland founded

1972 . . . . .BMC takes over administration of MLTB training schemes

. . . . .Ownership of Plas y Brenin changes from CCPR to Sports Council

1975 . . . . .First ascent of Everest by Britons, via North West face

. . . . .Association of Mountain Guides established

1976 . . . . .Bill March appointed Director of Plas y Brenin

. . . . .BMC adopts Hunt Report on Mountain Training

. . . . MLTB rejects Hunt Report on Mountain Training causing a rift between the organisations

1977 . . . . .John Barry appointed Director of Plas y Brenin

. . . . .ABMG becomes part of the Union Internationale des Associations des Guides de Montagne

1979 . . . . .MLTB reconstituted following settlement of dispute with BMC

1985 . . . . .Dave Alcock appointed Director of Plas y Brenin

1995 . . . . .Martin Doyle appointed Director of Plas y Brenin

1997 . . . . .Iain Peter appointed Chief Executive Officer of Plas y Brenin

Heads of Centre

G I "Gim" Milton . . . . .1955 -1960

John "Jacko" Jackson . . . . .1960 -1976

Bill March . . . . .1976 -1977

John Barry . . . . .1978 -1985

Dave Alcock . . . . .1985 -1995

Martin Doyle . . . . .1995 -1996

Iain Peter . . . . .1997 - 2006

Martin Doyle . . . . .2006 -

Chairman of the Management and Advisory Committees

Lord Hunt of Llanfair Waterdine .... 1955 -1965

Sir Jack Longland .... 1965 -1980

John Disley .... 1980 -1985

Alan Blackshaw .... 1985 -1996

Tim Marshall 1996-

Directors of the Mountain Training Trust

The MTT Board consists of a representative, preferably officers, from the BMC, MLTUK and MLTE with the option for one independent Director. At present the Chairman is in addition to, rather than drawn from, the other Directors

George Band (BMC) (Chairman 1996 - 1999)

Bob Barton (UKMTB)

Pete Butler (UKMTB)

Brian Griffiths (MLTE) (Chairman 2005 -)

Doug Jones (MLTB, MLTUK)

Aly Kellas (MLTB) (Vice Chairman 1999 - 2002)

Nick Kempe (UKMTB)

John Mackenzie (MC of S)

Dave Musgrove (BMC)

Kate Ross (MLTS)

Dawson Stelfox (UKMTB)

Mark Vallance (BMC)

Derek Walker (BMC Chairman 2002 - 2005)